MURDER & MAYHEM
—— IN ——
ERIE, PENNSYLVANIA

MURDER & MAYHEM
— IN —
ERIE, PENNSYLVANIA

JUSTIN DOMBROWSKI

THE
History
PRESS

Published by The History Press
Charleston, SC
www.historypress.com

First published 2022

ISBN 978-1-5402-5252-4

Library of Congress Control Number: 2022933328

CONTENTS

ACKNOWLEDGEMENTS

Writing this book proved to be a more monumental task than originally envisioned. There are many individuals who helped see this project to completion, and I am forever indebted to their assistance. I wish to thank J. Banks Smither, acquisition editor for The History Press, who made himself available at all times to ensure that the vision for this book came to realization.

Chief of Police Dan Spizarny and Sergeant Stan Tuznik with the Erie City Police Department provided clarification in regards to the police department's criminal records.

Austin Brugger and Brugger Funeral Home were kind enough to share and grant permission to use a photograph of Brugger's Undertaking Parlor when it was located on East Ninth Street. Beth Jacobs, great-niece of Erie police officer Magnus Jensen, and her family were gracious in allowing the usage of a photograph of Officer Jensen.

Richard Cowell Esq., a longtime family friend, was always generous with his thoughts and perspectives on Erie history.

Members of Brith Sholom Erie, Erie's Conservative Jewish congregation, were both gracious and kind with my questions about burial procedures in the local Brith Sholom Cemetery. David Lester, the cemetery vice-president, was knowledgeable and answered my endless questions, especially with explaining the Jewish customs that would have occurred surrounding Rachel's burial.

Erie County Historical Society director George Deutsch and his staff have been supportive since the early stages of this project. George provided every resource available to ensure that this collection of tales would cement itself in the annals of Erie County's colorful history. Archivist Pauline Stanton was both knowledgeable and helpful in locating documents and photographs pertinent to the source material. Without their support, certain portions of this book could not have been possible.

My father, Gary Dombrowski, provided the illustrations of various maps throughout the book and jumped at the opportunity to help. My mother, Julie, has provided her support since the earliest inception of this project.

Finally, this book would not have become reality without the support of my children, Sierra, Sophia and Benjamin, for the moments where this book sometimes pulled me away from daily life. And lastly, I could not have done this book without the support of my wife, Sara, who endured endless lonely nights and weekends while her husband was off chasing ghosts of the past.

INTRODUCTION

T he Pizza Bombing Case of 2003. The suicide of Facebook Killer Steve Stephens. The 1990 murder trial of Dr. John Boyle. Such stories have made headlines around the world, introducing millions of viewers to the shores of Erie, Pennsylvania.

In Erie, however, it is a different tale. The horrific and macabre scenes that flourish through Erie County are not new. Ask anyone who has lived here, and you'll be fed stories of sex, drugs, murder and, most importantly, mystery.

Stories that will be burned into your memory forever.

The infamous 1988 murder of Janine Kirk, found buried on the beaches of Presque Isle. The unsolved murder of Tammy Pelc, buried in the basement of an apartment building—found only when the smell of decomposing flesh led to her discovery. The still unsolved murder of Corporal Robert Owens of the Erie City Police Department. The eerie Presque Isle UFO sighting of 1966. The Legend of Ax-Murder-Hollow.

The list goes on and on.

Oh, and did you know that the Mafia has discarded their victims in Misery Bay? It's true, some claim.

It was about fourteen years ago, while I was studying criminal justice at Mercyhurst University, that local crimes reported on the internet piqued my curiosity. What other cases are there out there from Erie's history? Not just any cases. Older cases. A visit to Blasco Memorial Library revealed some clues or into some of Erie's older crimes.

True crime has become a popular topic for armchair investigators. There's an unexplainable thrill to digging into the crimes of the past, into other worlds, almost, in an attempt to succeed where others have failed. Anyone who is fascinated by older crimes will tell you there's a certain addiction that accompanies it.

Writing a book about Erie County's most infamous and unsolved older crimes was not something I was prepared for, but the curiosity within me continued to persist. So, I dug deeper.

Case files from cases prior to 1945 no longer exist within the Erie City Police Department. For some of the cases that involved some of Erie's older unsolved murders, such as that of Manley W. Keene and Rachel Levin, the autopsies of those victims have not survived and were pieced together from portions of newspaper clippings that quoted inquest testimonies.

Then there was the arduous task of reviewing microfilm from Erie's major newspapers at the time: the *Erie Daily Times* and the *Dispatch-Herald*.

The majority of information revealed in this book, in addition to newspaper articles, comes from records within the Courthouse Archives at the Erie County Historical Society, some ranging from the mid- to late 1800s to about roughly the mid-1950s. Within these files were criminal cases that were tried by the district attorney at that time. These files are accompanied with a docket entry and would also possibly include an inquest transcript or a transcript for a preliminary hearing. Most of the court trial transcripts prior to 1950 have not survived; however, there are still some that can be found.

With most of the cases in this book being over one hundred years old, additional evidence and information was difficult to come by when it came to my research.

Another challenge was identifying the locations of the crimes from Erie's past. Most are almost unrecognizable. Others have been lost to history forever.

I also used my ten-plus years as a genealogist to help further reveal the lives of those involved. Technology is a great tool for investigating the past, and much information was obtained from different sources throughout the country with access that detectives and reporters from back then could have only dreamed of.

Included in this book are numerous photographs, maps and firsthand accounts to present an in-depth narrative for the reader. These, along with newspaper articles and my research of fourteen-plus years, provide an opportunity to piece together crimes for the first time in almost a century. *Murder and Mayhem in Erie, Pennsylvania* is a time machine that allows you, the reader and armchair investigator or historian, to go back in time and relive the tragedies that shaped Erie's history. Whether you're a true crime aficionado or interested in local Erie history, there is something here for everyone.

Oh, and I must digress—I have yet to come across conclusive proof that victims of Erie's rumored Mafia were discarded in Misery Bay.

But you never know.

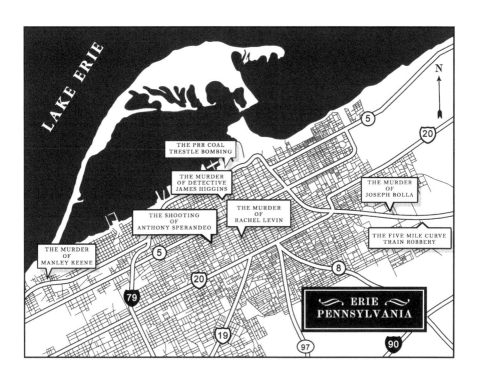

LAKE ERIE

N

THE PRR COAL
TRESTLE BOMBING

THE MURDER
OF DETECTIVE
JAMES HIGGINS

THE MURDER
OF
JOSEPH BOLLA

THE SHOOTING
OF
ANTHONY SPERANDEO

THE MURDER
OF
RACHEL LEVIN

THE FIVE MILE CURVE
TRAIN ROBBERY

THE MURDER
OF
MANLEY KEENE

ERIE
PENNSYLVANIA

1

DEAD AT THE POST OF DUTY

The 1905 Murder of Detective Sergeant James Higgins

B y all accounts, the early morning hours of Sunday, May 14, 1905, were uneventful for the Erie City Police Department. Most of the officers on duty were already patrolling the streets and answering calls. It was just past 1:00 a.m.[1] when the police received a call from Martin Grass, night watchman at the Henry Shenk Company Mill on the corner of West Twelfth and Sassafras Streets. Grass reported a suspicious person was seen loitering in the area.

With all available officers absent, Detective Sergeant James "Jimmy" Higgins promptly responded to the call and left the station on his bicycle, venturing up Sassafras Street, where he performed a careful examination of the premises around the Henry Shenk Company Mill. Finding no evidence of suspicious persons, Higgins returned to police headquarters in less than a half an hour.[2]

Higgins, returning to his desk, came to the conclusion he was not satisfied with his inspection. "By gum, John I believe I'll take another look around up there."[3] Higgins remarked to Officer John Fletcher.

Higgins spoke with Captain William J. Detzel, telling him he was going to make his way back to the Shenk Mill for another inspection.

"If there is any call and you want me, come out Seventh and up Sassafras Street, and you will meet me," Higgins told Officer Fletcher. Higgins passed Desk Officer John Hagerty, left headquarters at 1:38 a.m. and proceeded back to the premises of Henry Shenk Company Mill. Arriving at the mill, Higgins performed another inspection, again finding no suspicious persons.

Satisfied with his additional search, Higgins started out, traveling north on Sassafras Street to head back to headquarters. Upon reaching the intersection of West Eleventh and Sassafras, Higgins turned his attention to Central High School and observed someone standing inside the entrance.

Higgins dismounted his bicycle and approached the individual.

"What are you doing there?" the detective called out.

A man exited the entrance, coming down the stairs.

"Who are you?" the stranger asked.

"A special officer. I won't hurt you," Higgins responded reassuringly.

As the policeman came within a few feet of the man, a gunshot rang out and a bullet entered Higgins's jaw.

"Murder!" screamed Higgins as he lunged forward, grabbing the man before both became entangled in a ferocious struggle. As Higgins fought for the weapon, the attacker pressed the gun against Higgins's body and fired twice more. Higgins slumped to the ground, his hands still clasped in a death grip on the man's coat. Shedding the coat, the gunman fled south on Sassafras Street, disappearing into the darkness.

Central High School. *Author's collection.*

Wilhelmina Doll, at 1022 Sassafras Street, heard the gunshots while taking care of one of her sick children. Doll notified her husband, Conrad, who in turn called police headquarters.

Within minutes, phone calls started to trickle in.

"That must be Jimmy Higgins!" said Captain Detzel to Detective Richard Crotty, and soon both men were pedaling their bicycles south on Sassafras Street to Central High School. The men pedaled past the darkened silhouette of St. Peter's Cathedral and immediately noticed a crowd of people near the entrance of the high school—accompanied by the moans of the dying Higgins.

As Crotty and Detzel approached the crowd, they saw that Higgins was lying on his side, his arm resting underneath his head for support. Immediately, a call was placed for Berkenkamp's ambulance. While they waited, those around Higgins did the most they could to make him comfortable. A bloodstained overcoat, which Higgins's killer had discarded, was found nearby, partly under the wire netting around a flower bed.

Detective Crotty knelt down next to Higgins.

"Jimmy, are you shot?"

"I'm all in." Higgins replied weakly.

When asked, Higgins was able to provide a brief description of his attacker. The man who shot him was "young, dressed in a dark suit with a sack coat. He wore a derby hat. His hair was red, and he was of medium build with a slightly flushed face."[4]

Around this moment, Detectives John T. Grant and Henry Freund arrived on scene. Higgins asked Detective Crotty for a priest, and the detective immediately sped to the nearby parochial residence of St. Peter's Cathedral. After the felled officer asked for his wife, Detective Freund left for the Higgins residence.

A reporter from the *Erie Daily Times* described the crime scene in detail:

> At the north side of the path leading to the main entrance of the school there is a bed of shrubs protected by a wire netting about 33 inches high. At this place the struggle between the officer and his murderer took place. The ground in the bed was tramped down and indented as if by the fall of a heavy body and one of the largest plants had blood stains on it. Just outside of the wire netting the officer lay in a pool of blood and his feet and shoe laces were entangled in the wire.[5]

Within minutes, the ambulance arrived, and those around Higgins began the careful task of placing him inside. Detective Crotty cradled Higgins's head as he was being lifted into the ambulance. Those present were then greeted suddenly by Father John Donnellan, who offered a quick prayer.

The ambulance left and arrived at Hamot Hospital at 2:30 a.m. Higgins was attended to by hospital surgeon Dr. Francis Goeltz and was joined soon by his wife and children.

Dr. Goeltz performed a quick examination of Higgins and determined the wounds to be fatal. Later, Dr. Goeltz would recall the first bullet entered Higgins's right lower jaw, which "shattered the lower edge of the lower jaw; was deflected to the throat; perforated the upper part of the windpipe and lodged in the throat; there were powder marks on the face, nose and ear."[6]

Detective Sergeant Richard T. Crotty. *From the* Erie Daily Times.

In regard to the two gunshot wounds that followed, these were "3¼ inches below the right nipple, which shattered the rib; went through and shattered the liver; through the right kidney and the muscles of the back. The other was 1½ inches below, through the abdominal wall, pancreas and left kidney; the abdominal cavity was filled with blood."[7]

Upon Dr. Goeltz's examination, Father Peter Cauley of St. Patrick's Church was sent for, along with local Dr. George B. Kalb. Accompanied by Alderman Clark M. Cole, Captain Detzel arrived at Hamot Hospital and was informed that Higgins would not survive.

Detective Sergeant John T. Grant. *From the* Erie Daily Times.

Taking charge of the investigation, Captain Detzel notified every available officer about the shooting. Officers were ordered to double up along the railroads and Union Depot and a description of Higgins's attacker was subsequently telephoned and telegraphed to all surrounding towns and cities. Additional inquiries were led by Detective Grant, who set out for "Sassafras Street with a squad of men as quickly as he could get around."[8]

While officers of the Erie City Police Department hunted Higgins's attacker, Detzel had the foresight to get a statement from Higgins. With Higgins's condition rapidly deteriorating, Captain Detzel and Alderman Cole attempted to obtain a statement. The *Erie Daily Times* described the atmosphere:

> *The death bed scene was a touching one. Mrs. Higgins was nearly frantic and there was not a dry eye in the room, accustomed as nurses and attendants are to such scenes, as the wife and children and fellow officers knelt with the priest around the bed.*[9]

Detzel started to speak to Higgins but was cautioned by Father Cauley to speak louder.

"Do you know me?" Detzel asked, leaning over Higgins.

"Billy…" Higgins responded feebly.

"Was the man who shot you old?" No answer.

"Was he young?" Detzel continued.

Higgins nodded yes.

"How dressed; light?" No answer.

"Dark?"

Higgins nodded yes, again.

"Light or dark? Dark?" There was no answer.

"Light?"

"Yes," Higgins responded, "Red-headed."[10]

Alderman Cole then presented a paper, and Higgins made his mark. Ten minutes later, Detective Sergeant James "Jimmy" Higgins slipped into unconsciousness and succumbed to his injuries at 3:31 a.m. He was fifty-eight years old.

A City in Mourning

James Higgins was born in November 1847 in Buffalo, New York—the second oldest of four children—to Martin and Sarah Higgins,[11] who had emigrated from Ireland. In the 1860s, Higgins worked as a laborer in the city of Buffalo before moving to Erie in 1870. In 1871, Higgins married Johanna McDonnell in Erie, Pennsylvania, and worked as a sailor on the Great Lakes during the summer months and saltwater fished during the winter.

Detective Sergeant James Higgins. *Courtesy of the Erie City Police Department.*

On July 4, 1881, James Higgins was appointed to the Erie City Police Department by Mayor Joseph McCarter. Higgins would rise through the ranks, being promoted to roundsman and finally detective sergeant in 1895. He was known as "one of the kindest and gentlest of characters"[12] and well regarded in the police department and the community. Higgins was known to not use his revolver, except as a case of last resort. "I won't ever kill anyone; Nobody would ever shoot me,"[13] he remarked on one occasion.

Higgins was also involved in some of the more high-profile criminal cases of the day in Erie, such as the capture and arrest of Christian Schau in 1886[14] and the arrest, with then Detective Sergeant William Detzel, of George Bonier at the Morton House in 1903.[15]

At the time of his death, James Higgins had been married to Johanna for thirty-four years, and their marriage had produced seven children: four sons (Thomas, John, James and Joseph) and three daughters (Sarah, Marie and Helen). He was also a grandfather to James and Kathleen.

Recorded as the first Erie City police officer killed in the line of duty, the death of Detective Sergeant James Higgins was met with widespread grief on the morning of May 14, 1905. Father Cauley of St. Patrick's Church was said to have been so distraught by the events that he was unable to serve mass that day, and the crime scene in front of Central High School was "visited during the day by thousands."[16]

Both of Erie's leading newspapers—the *Erie Daily Times* and the *Erie Dispatch*—called for the police to hunt Higgins's killer at all costs, to the edges of the earth if need be. Higgins's death left his widow, Johanna Higgins, hardly able to care for her children. The *Erie Daily Times* stepped up and proposed a memorial fund:

> *James Higgins lost his life in YOUR service. In protecting YOUR homes and YOUR lives from harm. Shall it be said that any one of us could not and would not give one dollar for a fund to be presented to his widow? The* Times *places the answer right up to the people whom James Higgins has been faithfully serving for nearly twenty-five years. Let them answer.*[17]

And answer the citizens of Erie did—they went on to raise $1,040. In addition to the *Times*'s Memorial Fund, Mayor Robert J. Saltsman started a fund for the Higgins family. The generosity of Erie's citizens did not go unnoticed, which was evident in the Higginses' statement in response: "It is the greatest consolation to know, at a time when the deepest gloom pervades our home, that he who was most dear to us, was honored and appreciated by the good people he had long and faithfully served."[18]

The grief and sadness of Higgins's death even affected those in the Erie County Jail when Warden John Butler announced the news that morning; the announcement was met with "the deepest regret for the sad affair."[19] Even criminals expressed respect for the humility and life of Detective Sergeant Higgins and offered their services to hunt Higgins's murderer. While many grieved that morning over Higgins's death, the hunt for his killer continued.

The Manhunt Begins

Erie City Police attempted to head off Higgins's murderer from escaping through the railroads, but it was widely believed that the killer—whoever he was—was already long gone. Speculation had also begun sifting through press reports, claiming the killer was captured in the nearby borough of Girard and as far away as Ashtabula, Ohio. Eventually, these reports were proven false, but they added drama to the opening stages of the investigation.

For Erie County detective Frank H. Watson, the hunt for Higgins's killer was personal. "I was anxious from the start to do all that I could to run down the murderer of Jimmie Higgins,"[20] Watson would later recall. Forty-nine-year-old Detective Watson's reputation was well known throughout Erie County. An Erie native, Watson had worked for both the railroad and Erie City Police prior to being appointed as county detective three years earlier by Erie County District Attorney Milton W. Shreve. Watson was known to maintain a tight lid on his investigations, something that irritated local reporters, and he was also known to go toe-to-toe with those he disagreed with. And on the morning of Higgins's murder, Watson wasted no time in getting down to business.

After conferring with Chief of Police Edward Wagner, both men turned their attention to the evidence that was available to them. Confident that an overcoat found at the scene was from Higgins's killer, police searched the inside pockets and discovered a bottle opener and a handkerchief marked with a number. Also recovered at Central High School was a burglar's jimmy.[21] Police located the owner of the coat, identified as belonging to Hudson H. Hearns, 144 West Sixth Street. Hearns informed police that the coat, along with a box and a half of cigars and a valise containing pantaloons and underclothing, had been stolen from his residence on May 13.

Hearns also notified police that when his items were stolen from his residence the burglar's old clothing was left behind. When police inspected the clothing, they discovered they were at a disadvantage, as the prior owner had already taken steps to disguise the items before discarding them. The only additional clue was a pin under the lapel of the old coat—a pin that said "Central High School."

Watson was of the opinion that Higgins's attacker was the Hearns burglar, as similar cigars had been found at the entrance of Central High School. Watson also believed Higgins's murderer likely had an accomplice and that the murderer had been acting as a lookout while his partner was casing other neighborhoods in the nearby area. Hearns's missing valise was located and returned later that day.[22]

Central High School principal John Diehl contacted Detective Watson and notified him that the auditorium and a classroom had been entered. A case had been broken into, but nothing appeared to have been stolen.

As County Detective Watson ran down leads in and around Erie, Detective Sergeants Grant and Crotty took the early morning Nickel Plate train to Girard to investigate reports that a man matching the description of Higgins's murderer had gotten off a train in the general vicinity of the nearby Bessemer Junction. Crotty and Grant eventually obtained an automobile and tracked the suspicious man to a nearby hotel.

Upon entering the house, Crotty and Grant ordered the man to get out of bed and get dressed. Both detectives noted almost immediately that the man did not entirely match the description issued of Higgins's killer. Initially, the man was bewildered and unable to recall what occurred the night before and had cuts on his face and hands. But he was able to remember that he had in fact been in Erie the previous night and arrived in Girard aboard the trolley line. The man claimed he had been walking on the tracks when he picked up a bottle and threw it, breaking the bottle and cutting his hand. A ticket in his pocket corroborated his statement, and after the man was identified, the detectives were concerned he was not associated with the death of Higgins.[23]

As Detectives Crotty and Grant set out on foot toward nearby Fairview, dark clouds rolled across the landscape amid flashes of lightning and thunder that shook the countryside. Both men proceeded through a downpour as they examined every barn, shack and house they came across. Upon arriving at Fairview, both men took a trolley back to Erie that afternoon and reported to Chief Wagner, exhausted and empty-handed.

The inquest into the murder of James Higgins was held at 4:00 p.m. that day at the undertaking rooms of W.J. Quinn, at the corner of East Fifth and French Streets, presided over by Coroner John W. Schmelter. After viewing the remains of Detective Higgins at his residence, Coroner Schmelter began the proceedings.

The first witness called was Detective Crotty, who had just returned from his trip with Detective Grant to Girard. Crotty testified that he left the police station around 1:00 a.m. and had been speaking with Officer William Brown at the intersection of West Eighth and Myrtle Streets when he heard a gunshot, followed by two more. Crotty made his way to State Street and West Eighth, believing the shots had originated there, before returning to the police station. There he was informed of the shooting at Central High School, and he then proceeded to the school and spoke with Higgins before he was transferred to Hamot Hospital.

Next was Conrad Doll, who testified he was asleep in bed when he heard the first shot, followed by a cry of "Murder!" Doll then phoned the police

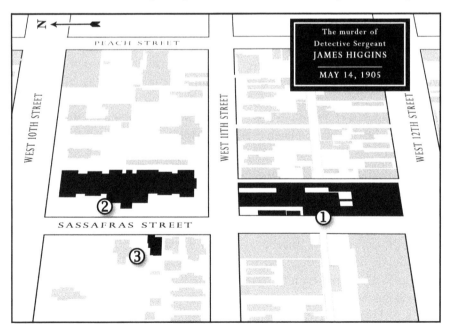

Map showing the vicinity of the (1) Henry Shenk Company Mill, (2) Central High School and the (3) Conrad Doll residence.

at 2:00 a.m. and claimed he could hear Higgins moaning, followed by the sound of a man's whistle.

Dr. Goeltz, who tended to Higgins upon his arrival at Hamot Hospital, provided clues from his autopsy report, which has not survived, followed by the testimony of Doctor Kalb, who also inspected Higgins at Hamot Hospital.

The jury returned a verdict that James Higgins was murdered by a person or persons unknown. They also offered the following recommendation: "We find the practice of sending one officer alone to investigate any attempted burglaries or arrest any suspicious character is unsafe and should not be allowed. Had another officer been with Officer Higgins, this crime would not have been committed."[24]

Later that night, the Erie County commissioners, along with both city and county councils, passed a resolution offering $2,000 for the capture of Higgins's killer. Mayor Saltsman used the opportunity to present his concerns regarding the number of available officers in the Erie City Police Department. Saltsman said Erie was "overrun with disreputable characters; that Erie had one policeman per 1,500 people"[25] and compared it to cities like Pittsburgh and New York City, where departments had a greater number of officers per citizen. Saltsman's request for the department to be increased to sixty men was referred to the police committee for further review.

It didn't take long for County Detective Watson to get on the murderer's trail, and this became clear on May 16, when a particular arrest of a burglar sent him on a search into Erie's criminal underworld. On May 11, 1905, a tramp sailor known as Robert M.A. Bowen had been arrested after breaking into the parishes of St. Stanislaus and Sacred Heart. In questioning Bowen, Watson heard that he had been in the recent company of a well-known local criminal, James "Freck" McCarthy.

When questioned by Watson, Bowen had already pleaded guilty to larceny and breaking and entering and was awaiting his turn to be transported to the Allegheny County Workhouse. Bowen confirmed to Watson that he had met McCarthy on about May 10 at the Hoffman house bar. McCarthy was in the company of another man, described as "about 20 or 25 years old, smooth face, about 5 feet 6 inches in height and weighs about 160 pounds."[26] The other man introduced himself as Frank Connor.

It was his belief, Bowen told Watson, that McCarthy and Connor were acquainted with each other. Connors was apparently from Flint, Michigan, and had mentioned to McCarthy he planned to stay around Pennsylvania before traveling into Ohio and then Wisconsin. Detective Higgins passed the window at some point, according to Bowen, and McCarthy stated, "I'll never do another two years or 18 months again in a hurry. That damn Higgins is the cause of me and a few more getting pinched."[27]

This prompted a response from Connors, who replied, "Well, if he ever comes near me I won't give him time or any other. I'll just drop them for good."[28]

Later, the three men crossed the Lake Shore & Michigan Southern Railroad tracks and entered another saloon. It was here that Bowen spoke to Connors further until they were interrupted by McCarthy, who schemed a plan to break into St. Stanislaus Roman Catholic Church. Their escape, if needed, would be made possible, according to McCarthy, with some nitroglycerine. Later that night, Bowen was arrested, and McCarthy and Connors escaped. Bowen believed that either McCarthy or Frank Connors was responsible for Higgins's death.

Upon questioning Bowen and learning information that seemed to point in the direction of Higgins's killer, Watson later privately confided in both Commissioner Norman McLallen and John Callaghan, editor of the *Erie Daily Times*, that he was confident that he knew who killed Detective Higgins. Watson asked both men to keep the developments from the public, and both indicated they would not interfere with the investigation.

Detective Watson was confident that he knew the identity of the murder, now all he had to do was find him.

REQUIEM FOR GOD'S DUTY

At eight o'clock on the morning of May 16, 1905, Chief Edward Wagner and Captain William Detzel marched from city hall leading a silent column of police officers in a procession to the residence of Detective Higgins. Almost the entire police force, those who could be "spared from their posts," were present in full uniform.

Despite the request from the Higgins family that flowers be omitted, the *Erie Daily Times* reported a "profusion of beautiful floral pieces, prominent among which were a broken circle from the police force, bearing a long white streamer with the legend, 'Brother Officers,' and a bed of American Beauty roses from the Erie Chamber of Commerce."[29]

The Higgins residence was full to capacity of sympathizers. Next to the casket, the Higgins family looked on, keeping watch. It was said that many of the elder police officers and those who served alongside Higgins openly

Present-day view of the Higgins residence (*far left*) and St. Patrick's Roman Catholic Church. *Author's collection.*

wept.[30] Soon the lid to the casket was shut and removed from the residence as officers lined up on both sides of the sidewalk, stretching in a line to nearby St. Patrick's Church. Chief Wagner, Captain Detzel, Detective Crotty, former captain Thomas Culhane and Fire Chief John McSullivan served as pallbearers.

Inside the entrance to St. Patrick's Church, ushers greeted the mourners at the front doors and seated attendees, which included prominent city and county officials. Soon every seat was accounted for. and "hundreds of friends of the deceased were turned away on account of the lack of the room."[31]

Reverend Peter Cauley, said to be "garbed in the vestments of the deepest mourning," delivered the eulogy, recalling the life of Detective Higgins. Cauley praised Higgins's Christian principles, character and loyalty as well as his respect for the rule of law. Cauley spoke, more importantly, of Higgins's desire to forgive his murderer. In closing, Cauley remarked:

> *You have known Mr. Higgins, or was he more commonly known as "Jimmy,"*
> *I hope you will remember him; remember him as he was—the faithful, the*
> *true and efficient officer who had the interests of the city at heart, and who*
> *fully realized the obligations he owed to the city for what he obtained.*[32]

Following the funeral service, a special trolley car carried police officers to Trinity Cemetery on West Lake Road. A steady procession of carriages followed the body, and upon arriving at the cemetery, officers formed in double lines before the grave. Soon the body of Detective-Sergeant James Higgins was laid to eternal rest.

In the days and weeks that followed, there was no shortage of suspects, despite Detective Watson's belief he was closing in on the killer. The suspects—most of whom were arrested due to having red hair—caused speculation to explode throughout the nearby cities and towns

Reverend Peter Cauley.
From the Erie Daily Times.

and even into New York and Ohio. This was apparent by a headline in the *Erie Dispatch* on May 20, 1905, that was succinct and to the point: "Red Haired Men Must Watch Out."

Suspects were arrested in Dunkirk, New York. Police in Meadville believed that they had captured Higgins's killer. There was even a case in New Castle, outside of Pittsburgh, where police arrested two men who fit the description of Higgins's killer. All these leads, although scrutinized and investigated, were, unbeknownst to reporters and other authorities, actually nothing more than red herrings.

Weeks turned into months without any leads. That was, until June 24, 1905.

A reporter for the *Erie Daily Times* wrote that during the early morning hours of June 24, 1905, County Detective Watson and Councilman Charles Franklin were spotted exiting a westbound train with a short redheaded man in handcuffs. Both men attempted to keep the prisoner out of sight and hurried him from the depot to the Erie County Jail. The rumored identity of the man was none other than James "Freck" McCarthy, who was reported to have been arrested and interrogated in Buffalo, New York.

The reporter, writing from Jamestown, New York, further asked why there was such little reporting in the Higgins murder case:

> *The newspapers have been unjustly censured because so little has been said concerning a matter of so great moment. It is a recognized fact that in order to accomplish the best results in criminal detection it must be done quietly. From the start County Detective Watson and all the other officials in the case have kept "mum" and on different occasions, when rumors were afloat*

regarding certain movements of the officers, the reporters were asked to assist the detectives by withholding the information.[33]

This article also raises some interesting details. It is known that several days following the murder, McCarthy was already on Watson's radar. Also, from past instances, Watson was familiar with McCarthy and his criminal background. Whether the man was in fact McCarthy is not known, as Watson never discussed this part of the investigation, but the article seems to be support the idea that Watson had in fact arrested McCarthy and subjected him to questioning pertinent to the Higgins murder.

As for Freck McCarthy, his luck would soon run out.

On August 2, 1905, a Lake Shore Railroad section gang located the mutilated remains of a man lying next to the tracks three miles west of the North Springfield Station. The man, who had red hair and a red-colored moustache, had apparently fallen from the train. When the section gang came across the body, they noted the back of his head had been smashed in. Detective Watson, assisted by Councilman Franklin, left for Springfield.

Near the spot where the body was located, a youth named Roy Conroy of Youngstown, Ohio, told railroad workers that the dead man was Mike Flynn or Mike Welsh, who, he claimed, was wanted by the Erie City Police. Conroy was then detained until Watson and Franklin's arrival.

When Watson and Franklin arrived, they learned the remains had been photographed before a prompt burial. Upon reviewing the photographs, Watson was certain the dead man was none other than Freck McCarthy.[34] Three months had passed since Higgins's death, and it appeared that Watson was no longer of the opinion McCarthy was Higgins's killer. This was supported by the fact that Higgins had recalled prior to his death that the man was a stranger to him. Watson's attention still zeroed in on Frank Connors from Michigan.

As the end of summer of 1905 was in sight, there was a growing mood that Detective Higgins's killer would never be apprehended. This would change when Detective Watson received a telegraph from Columbus, Ohio. The police there claimed that they had someone in custody who they believed was Higgins's killer.

It was Frank Connors—and he had killed another police officer.

A Suspect Is Arrested

On the night of June 7, 1905, the Columbus Police Department was notified of a break-in at the home of Horace L. Chapman, 1111 East Broad Street.[35] The Columbus Police, on high alert due to reported burglaries there several nights prior, sprang into action and, within a short amount of time, surrounded the mansion. Officers entered, surprising the burglars, and a chase ensued throughout the home. The burglars were frantically moving from room to room, slamming the doors behind them as they desperately tried to escape. The thieves then exited the building, making their way to a shed located next to a high board fence in the rear of the home. One of the burglars exited through the shed window and leapt over the fence.

The burglar was suddenly face-to-face with Officer Daniel Davis. Before Davis could respond, he was shot in the stomach twice and killed instantly.[36] Upon hearing the shots, additional officers raced to the back of the house, but by this time, the burglar had fled after dropping his revolver.[37] Detective Henry James gave pursuit, catching up with the burglar several blocks away, striking him on the back of the head with his gun. Davis's killer was promptly handcuffed and taken to the Columbus Police Station, where he gave his name as Frank Conrad, twenty-three years old.

At the Columbus Police Station, Chief of Detectives James A. Dundon examined Conrad, who denied he shot Davis and denied ever being in the penitentiary. He also refused to confirm the identity of another man, named Reed, arrested shortly after the burglary.[38] Several days later, Dundon would learn that Conrad was not the man's true identity and dug further into the murderer's background. Conrad, who claimed he was a bartender working for an individual in Canton by the name of John O'Neil, also confirmed he went by the alias of Connors. But more importantly, his real name was Fred Caster.

The Life and Crimes of Fred Caster

Frederick Caster was born in 1877 in Cleveland, Ohio, to Amos and Margaret Caster. The family soon moved to Flint, Michigan. Not much is known about Caster's early years, but at some point he started to engage in petty crimes, which escalated throughout his later teenage years.

On May 13, 1902, in the small town of Bay City, Michigan, Caster burglarized a home, only to be recognized the afterward by Saginaw police officer Elmer E. Bishop. Bishop apprehended Caster and was in the process of transporting him to the police station when Caster pulled away from him, pulling a revolver on the officer. Both men engaged in a brief fight before Caster surrendered. He was later taken to the station, where he provided a false name—Frank Considine. Caster, then on parole from the Ionia Reformatory,[39] was found guilty on June 14, 1902, for the burglary as well as holding two boarders up at gunpoint. He was sentenced to the Michigan State Prison in Jackson, Michigan, for a term of six years.

Fred Caster's mug shot. *From the* Erie *Daily Times.*

Caster would escape from prison on June 23, 1904, and was never apprehended. He fled from Michigan, passing through Ohio, Pennsylvania and into New York. Authorities later discovered that at some point between his escape and capture in Officer Davis's death he had also served short stints in workhouses in Toledo and Cleveland.

Around the time of Freck McCarthy's demise, County Detective Watson had heard about Caster's arrest in Columbus and wrote to the chief of police there requesting a photograph, description and record of aliases. It was on August 18, 1905, that a small article in the *Cleveland Leader* attracted the attention of the *Erie Daily Times*:

> *Detective Frank Watson, of Erie, Pa., has written to Chief of Police O'Connor asking for a photograph and description record of aliases of Fred Castor, now in the county jail charged with the murder of Officer Dan Davis, during the attempt to burglarize the residence of Horace L. Chapman, wealthy coal operator and former Democratic Candidate for Governor.*[40]

The *Times* seized on the article and confronted Watson that morning. Surprised at the leak, Watson had no choice but to go public with a statement:

> *I realize fully the delicacy of the position in which I am placed. The public is anxious to know just what is being done, and while I am always willing to give out information, if possible, I feel that I cannot say a word, either denying or affirming any of the rumors afloat.*[41]

When questioned about his decision to keep quiet about the updates, Watson defended his investigation:

I am doing all in my power to ferret out the mystery surrounding the crime. The situation is such that I do not want to make a statement which might unduly excite the public or do anyone an injustice. I have worked harder and traveled more in the interests of this case than the public is aware of.[42]

As Watson plotted the next steps in his investigation, Fred Caster had no intentions of facing the electric chair. An informant placed in the Franklin County Jail by the sheriff produced several letters in which Caster had communicated to a man named Peter Mathias in Canton, asking for "soup, briars, a string, fuse and saws,"[43] in order to escape. On August 27, 1905, believing that Caster was going to attempt an escape, Sheriff George Karb placed several deputies around the county jail. Sure enough, the deputies came across several suspicious individuals and arrested them. In their possession was a package containing nitroglycerine.

It was reported that the nitroglycerine was so powerful that it would have been demolished a good portion of the county jail, killing most—if not all-of the prisoners inside, including Caster. The man arrested was James O'Brien, and police confirmed he had in fact been attempting to break free Fred Caster and Michael Murray.

Frank Watson and Chief Wagner left Erie on August 31, 1905, making several stops through various cities on the way to acquire additional information before arriving in Columbus. One of these stops was in Canton, Ohio. While in Canton, both men visited an individual by the name of Crowley. Crowley informed them that Caster had arrived there on May 16. Caster made the remark, "I done a dirty damn trick, this is the second man that I croaked and it is one of the regrets of my life. As this fellow rode up to me on a bicycle, I gave him a battle and he was the gamest man that I ever met and evidently was a good fellow."[44]

Crowley also revealed additional information that had not been made public in the press—information that was only known to the killer.

Watson and Wagner arrived in Columbus on September 1. The following day, they visited with Chief of Police O'Connor, Prosecutor Seymour and Sheriff Karb and discussed the Higgins and Davis cases. Columbus authorities pledged every avenue of assistance to Watson and Wagner. Watson asked and was granted permission to view the clothes Caster had on when arrested.[45] Armed with a description of clothing stolen from Hudson

Hearns on May 13, Watson believed he was viewing the same clothing. Watson was allowed to bring the clothes back to Erie for identification.

The most important task that Detective Watson would set out to accomplish was speaking to Caster himself. When granted permission to speak with Caster, both Watson and Wagner were escorted into the long, dark corridors of the basement of the Franklin County Jail where Caster was confined in a dark cell—commonly referred to as the dungeons.

As Wagner and Watson stood before the cell, a turnkey opened the door and Caster stepped into the corridor. He appeared to be nervous.

"How are you, Frank?" Watson asked, stepping forward and extending his hand. "How are you getting along?"

Caster's glare remained cast to the floor as he mumbled something about being abused. When he locked eyes with Wagner it appeared as if Caster had recognized him from somewhere. Viewing Caster in person, both Chief Wagner and Detective Watson confirmed that they had seen Caster before as well.

"Frank, I came up to see if you would do me a favor. I have a very important question to ask you, which I would very much like to have you answer, if you feel it would not be injuring your case?"

"Well, what is it?" Caster asked.

"I have reason to think that you can tell me where a certain valuable fur-lined coat is which was taken from Erie some time ago."

"I do not know," Caster responded, nervously but visibly excited, "I don't know anything about Erie and that settles it."

After several minutes, Watson was able to get Caster to calm down enough so he could continue his questioning. He continued, "Frank, you are not as fleshy as you were the last time I saw you."

"You don't know me," Caster responded.[46]

Although the discussion continued, it did not lead to a confession to the murder of Detective Higgins. But with the evidence accumulated since their departure from Erie, both Watson and Wagner were confident that Higgins's killer was Fred Caster. Hudson Hearns was asked to come to the county courthouse. Arriving at Watson's office, Hearns confirmed that Caster's clothes were the same articles of clothing that were stolen on May 13. Hearns described, in detail, the way the suit had been tailored and that it was specially ordered for thirty-three dollars from Brooks Brothers in New York City.

Upon the return of Chief Wagner and Detective Watson, both men had discovered that their recent trip created palpable excitement in Erie. The citizens who mourned Higgins's loss were eager to scarf up every bit of detail they could. Had Jimmy Higgins's killer finally been caught? Would he stand trial in Erie for the murder?

Watson responded to the excitement through the *Times*:

> *I am positive beyond the shadow of a doubt that Frank Connors is the man who murdered "Jimmie" Higgins. I have given you a large part of the evidence which we have against the man, but not all of it by any means. It would not be policy for me to do so at this time. It might happen that he would be released in the Ohio courts of the serious charge against him and if that should happen then we will need the evidence against him which we deem it best to reserve at this time. Should he be released in the Ohio courts he will be brought to Erie and put on trial, charged with the murder of Detective Higgins. If that happens and the jury do their duty we will give him the rope.*[47]

James O'Brien, Caster's friend who attempted to dynamite Caster to freedom in the nitroglycerine plot in Columbus, was found guilty in October 1905. Caster proceeded to trial in December, waiving his right to a jury trial. He pleaded guilty to the murder of Officer Daniel Davis. Newspapers anticipated a life sentence, with some claiming that it would be unlikely he would ever stand trial in Erie.[48]

On December 21, 1905, Fred Caster was sentenced to death by electrocution.

Immediately following his death sentence, Caster's defense attorneys filed numerous appeals in an attempt to prevent his execution. These attempts dragged on throughout much of 1906. By the fall of 1906, many doubted that Caster would ever go to the chair. The dragging of the appeals caused so much frustration that Martha Gibbons, a matron of the Columbus Police Department, asked to pull the switch herself.

"Castor has shown himself to be a villain," Gibbons said. "He holds human life as nothing if it stands in his way in practicing his unlawful occupation of robbery. Special efforts are being made to save the life of this man. All the state courts have been exhausted in his behalf and they are now talking of taking it to the Supreme Court of the United States. That is what stirs me up."[49]

By January 1907, despite numerous pleas from Caster's friends, family and attorneys, he had exhausted all avenues to prevent his inevitable date with the electric chair. Detective Watson, sensing that Caster's days were numbered, traveled again to Columbus toward the end of January, when the

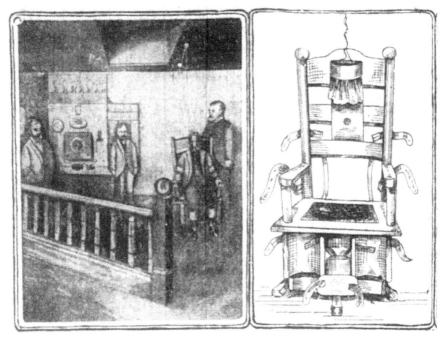

Condemned Man Just Before Electric
Current Was Turned On.

The Chair In Which He Paid Death
Penalty.

An artist's interpretation of Caster's last minutes alive and the chair he was electrocuted in.
From the Erie Daily Times.

two men had another conversation which would be their last. What Watson and Caster discussed remains unknown, as the case files no longer exist. Upon his return to Erie, Watson promised to reveal all once Caster was executed but did relate that during their conversation, Caster confirmed he was present in Erie at the time of Higgins's murder.

Two days after Watson's departure from Columbus, Governor Andrew L. Harris declared he would not issue another stay of execution. Additionally, the pardon board voted unanimously to refuse an offer of clemency. Caster's execution was set for February 15, 1907. Several days before the execution, Caster tried in vain to delay again by asking for another reprieve. Governor Harris was unmoved, declaring that justice had been delayed long enough and "the law should take its victim."[50]

At 12:03 a.m. on February 15, 1907, Fred Caster was electrocuted at the Ohio Penitentiary in Columbus, Ohio. He was pronounced dead at 12:10 a.m.

Following Fred Caster's execution, the murder of Detective Sergeant James Higgins disappeared from the pages of local newspapers. County

Detective Frank Watson kept his promise and provided a lengthy statement that appeared on the day of Caster's execution laying out the evidence against Caster. Caster, Watson claimed, was likely the individual responsible for the death of Jimmy Higgins, and although the case against Caster at the time was largely circumstantial, Watson claimed that Erie was prepared to prosecute Caster if he should "fall through the cracks" in Ohio.

County Detective Watson would go on to be involved in some of Erie's most infamous crimes and unsolved mysteries within the next decade, garnering both praise and criticism. James "Freck" McCarthy's body still lies buried somewhere in Springfield, a tragic anecdote in the Higgins case. Frederick Caster's body was interred in Mount Calvary Cemetery in Columbus, Ohio, unclaimed by family and friends.

The Higgins family would not remain untouched by tragedy, however, and on August 3, 1915, when the Millcreek Flood ravaged the city of Erie, Higgins's son John; his wife, Winifred; and their two children, James and Marion, were among its thirty-six fatalities. The Higgins residence, where a city turned out to remember the first officer killed in the line of duty, still stands at 118 East Fourth street. And towering nearby is the nearby parish of St. Patrick's Roman Catholic Church, still serving those in the local community.

Present-day view of where Central High School once stood. *Author's collection.*

Grave of Detective
Sergeant James Higgins.
Author's collection.

116 years later, however, the look of downtown Erie has changed drastically.

The Hearns residence at 144 West Sixth street is long gone. Central High School, where James Higgins was shot, did not survive either. Demolished in 1968, it is now a parking lot for the Mother Theresa Academy. St. Stanislaus Roman Catholic Church, which unwittingly played a crucial role in the investigation into Higgins's murder with the arrest of Robert M.A. Bowen, still stands guard over the old Polish neighborhood, its double light blue domes still visible on a clear day.

As for Detective Sergeant James Higgins, he rests in eternal slumber in Trinity Cemetery, located near Waldameer Park. Located toward the rear of the cemetery, far away from the noisy traffic of West Lake Road, his grave remains in a peaceful portion of the cemetery, interred next to his wife, Johanna, and several of their children.

On April 1, 2003, almost ninety-eight years after his death, Detective Sergeant James Higgins was awarded the Erie City Police Department's Medal of Honor. The award was presented to Higgins's last remaining relatives in Erie. And across from city hall, in Perry Square, stands a memorial in honor of local police officers killed in the line of duty.

Fraternal Order of Police
Memorial to Fallen Officers
across from Erie City Hall.
Author's collection.

It is almost certain that had authorities had access to forensic means available today, it would have been easy to determine if Fred Caster was Higgins's killer. The evidence seems to overwhelmingly confirm that he was the killer, although officially the case still remains unsolved 116 years later.

2

THE MADMAN OF WEST LAKE ROAD

Private Detective Mary E. Holland and
the Murder of Manley W. Keene

A faint fall breeze whistled through the fields and farmlands of Millcreek Township on the dark morning of October 23, 1909, as farmer Ira O. Wilkinson trotted along in his horse and produce wagon on West Lake Road, bound for the city of Erie. At the time, West Lake Road was unpaved and stretched beyond the city limits, passing numerous woodlots, fields and farms in outer Erie County.

Passing the farm of John Kelso at 6:00 a.m., Wilkinson reached a bend in the roadway. In the darkness, Wilkinson's attention was attracted to dark shape on the footpath to his left next to a fence. Coming closer, Wilkinson could see the shape was that of a man who appeared to either be drunk or asleep.

"Hey there!" Wilkinson called out from his wagon but received no response.

Stepping down from his wagon, Wilkinson approached the man, noting that his arms were lying alongside his body. The face of the man was sunk into the gravel footpath. Wilkinson grabbed the man's shoulders, lifting him slightly from the ground, and saw blood on the man's forehead and underneath his chin.[51] Rushing back to the wagon and grabbing the reins, Wilkinson made his way to the Albert Kelso (a cousin of John) farm four hundred feet away.

Wilkinson rapped his fist against the door of the Kelso home and was greeted by Albert's wife, Liviona. He informed her that he believed there was a dead man in the road and asked for her to call the police. After Wilkinson left, Liviona Kelso contacted a nearby farmer, Seth Baer, asking him to come

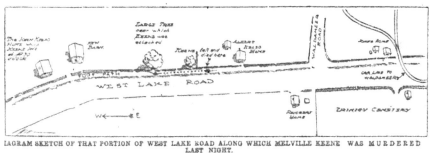

IAGRAM SKETCH OF THAT PORTION OF WEST LAKE ROAD ALONG WHICH MELVILLE KEENE WAS MURDERED LAST NIGHT.

Map of West Lake Road and nearby environs where Manley Keene was murdered, drawn by cartoonist Walter Kiedaisch. *From the* Erie Daily Times.

over. Baer soon arrived and confirmed there was a body on the footpath and identified him as Manley W. Keene, 109 West Third Street, a well-known carpenter from Erie.

When he arrived in Erie, Wilkinson also notified Erie County coroner Daniel Hanley. Hanley in turn notified County Detective Frank Watson, and both men sought the assistance of a local doctor, Wallace R. Hunter. Together they departed for the crime scene and were greeted with a horrific sight. Coroner Hanley approached the body and, upon turning it over, discovered numerous wounds. Furthermore, the throat had been cut.[52] Hanley finished a hasty examination and ordered Keene's remains removed to his undertaking rooms at 1228 Peach Street.

Detective Watson performed a quick inspection of the scene. Nearby, under a large chestnut tree, was a pool of blood, about one yard in diameter. A blood trail led to where the body had been found. Bloody shoeprints were also found.[53] The length from the chestnut tree to where the body was found measured roughly one hundred feet. A hickory club was also found halfway between the chestnut tree and the nearby residence of John Kelso.[54]

John Kelso, seventy-nine, confirmed to Watson that the victim was his cousin. Keene had visited his residence the night prior but left around 9:30 p.m. to catch the Waldameer trolley to his home in Erie. Kelso had tried to persuade Keene to stay, but Keene refused, telling him his wife would worry if he did not come home. Kelso mentioned that he stayed up for some time following Keene's departure and then went to bed. He reported hearing no suspicious noises and that his dog, asleep in the kitchen, had not noticed any disturbance.

While inspecting the exterior of Kelso's home, Watson noted there were drops of blood located on the veranda. The blood appeared as if someone had taken their hand, or an object, and flung blood from it. There was no blood on the nearby rug and front door of Kelso's veranda, which puzzled Watson and the other investigators. An extensive investigation yielded no other areas of blood.

The investigation had only been going on for several hours when Detective Watson was faced with more questions than answers. Meanwhile, in the city of Erie, Keene's son, John, was notified about the death of his father. Afterward, Keene broke the news to his mother and two sisters, who were "terribly broken up over the death of the husband father."[55]

Without an Enemy

Emmanuel Wesley Keene was born on October 9, 1859, in Flint, Michigan, to Francis and Harriet Keene. Keene's early years were spent in Michigan and Chicago. While serving aboard the tug *Alanson Summer*, Keene found his way to Erie; the tug operating in and around the harbor. It was when the tug was tied up in Erie during the winter months that Keene made Erie his home.

Manley W. Keene. *By Gary Dombrowski.*

Keene married Leona Raymond, daughter of Jacob Raymond, a well-known local marine engineer. Emmanuel, who went by the name "Manley," remained in Erie, and he continued the fishing business, even owning a tug until around 1894, when he became employed with Constable Brothers in Erie as a carpenter. Leona and Manley Keene had three children: John, Hazel and Grace.

The Keene family had not been immune to tragedy. This was clear in January 1909, when, while working at his residence, Keene fell from a stepladder. A chisel he had been holding penetrated his abdomen and intestines. Though the wound was initially believed to be fatal, Keene recovered; however, it would plague him for the rest of his life, leaving him rather weak and preventing him from continuing his trade as a carpenter. Eventually, Keene was promoted to the role of local business agent for Constable Brothers.

Keene's employers were shocked upon hearing the news of his death and told police Keene had no known enemies. He was considered intelligent and kept to himself. During his tenure as a local business agent, the Carpenters Union saw a rise in membership, due in part to Keene's "comprehensive conduct."[56]

The day before his death, it was union business that prompted Keene to travel to the John Kelso farm. He went to speak with carpenters and masons who were working on a new barn and repairing Kelso's house to encourage them to join the Carpenters Union. Keene's visit, according to Constable Brothers, was to "effect an understanding"[57] with the workers who were not members of the union.

Watson confirmed that Keene had stayed for supper, spending a portion of the evening with his cousins. He also had spoken to Seth Baer, a nearby farmer, that evening. In questioning Leona Keene, police learned that there were no indications of anything out of the ordinary and Keene informed his wife he would be back that evening.

Family and friends of Manley Keene were baffled as to who would butcher him—or why.

Hacked to Pieces

At his undertaking parlor, Coroner Hanley began the arduous task of performing an examination of Keene's body and the wounds inflicted. The wounds were more horrific than originally imagined, and the *Erie Dispatch* provided the grotesque details to its readers in full:

> *Seven wounds were found, one was a deep wound on the right side of the neck, between five and six inches long, which had severed the jugular vein. This wound was wide and gaping and exposed the windpipe, although it was not severed. It was three or four inches deep. But little blood flowed from this wound. Another deep wound, undoubtedly from the point of the instrument, was present on the inside of the left thigh, near the top. This wound penetrated the thigh about three and a half inches and severed the femoral artery. This wound, probably the first received by Keene, bled profusely, although less than two inches wide. His trousers and underwear were saturated by the flow from this incision which in itself would have been sufficient to have caused his death.*[58]

The *Dispatch* continued:

> *Between the left elbow and the armpit another wound about three and a half inches long, which penetrated into the muscles about an inch, was found. On the forearm of the same arm was another stab wound which was superficial, the arm apparently having been used to deflect a blow aimed for his body. Again this time, however, the knife reached its mark and penetrated the abdomen about three inches immediately below the spleen. Two wounds, from the point of the weapon, were found in the back over the region of the kidneys on the left side of the spine. These wounds were close together and penetrated to a depth of about two inches, and were apparently delivered while Keene was being pursued by his assailant. All of these wounds took effect through a heavy overcoat, a coat, vest, shirt and underwear.*[59]

Erie County coroner Daniel Hanley. *From the Erie Daily Times.*

Located in Keene's pockets were ten cents, a watch, and several letters, which were undisturbed. Upon inspecting Keene's vest, Hanley noted the buttons were missing. Robbery did not appear to be the motive, and Keene's body showed no signs of having been disturbed following the murder. But what caused the wounds?

Hanley thought it possible the wounds were inflicted by a large butcher knife, but these views changed after conferring with Dr. Hunter. After additional discussions, it was then believed the wounds were created by a corn knife or stiletto.

Ironically enough, although a detailed examination was performed, there was no autopsy. The body was then promptly prepared for burial and released to Keene's relatives.

THE INVESTIGATION CONTINUES

With the Keene investigation, County Detective Watson found himself in uncharted territory. Having been praised for his investigation into the murder of Detective Sergeant James Higgins in 1905, the years since had presented an altered landscape critical of both the Erie City Police Department and the county detective.

The early days of the Keene investigation saw Detective Watson refusing to make any statements about the case's status. At the outset, Watson did not appear concerned with the case, but the last thing he wanted was another unsolved murder like that of Anthony Bova[60] or the still then unsolved double homicide of Albert Damon and his sister, Jane Saterlee[61]—both cases that would be forever intertwined with Watson's legacy.

When approached by a reporter from the *Erie Daily Times* and asked if he was satisfied that he knew the identity of Keene's murderer, Watson responded that he did not who know the guilty party, "with a satisfied smile."[62]

MURDERED BY PARTY OR PARTIES UNKNOWN

Coroner Dan Hanley oversaw the inquest into the murder of Manley Keene at his undertaking rooms on the night of October 23, 1909. Those whose eyes were glued to the gory details of the murder in the *Times* and *Dispatch* were only further disappointed when the inquest failed to shed additional details. Ultimately, the inquest would add more questions about the growing mystery.

The first witness called was John Kelso, who repeated the story that he had relayed to Detective Watson. Keene had originally intended to take the 8:45 p.m. trolley at Waldameer to Erie but missed the trolley. Keene stayed until 9:30 and left at that time to catch the next trolley at 9:45 p.m. Kelso's daughter-in-law, Anna, was also present and bid Keene goodbye. The last Kelso saw of Keene was observing him walking east on West Lake Road heading toward Waldameer. Kelso and his daughter-in-law then went inside and shut the door.

Anna Kelso was the next witness called and corroborated her father-in-law's statement. Additional witnesses were Ira Wilkinson and Seth Baer. The final witness called was Detective Watson, who would only discuss the distance between the large pool of blood found next to the chestnut tree and Keene's body. Watson's responses, which were evasive, confirmed that he believed that the bloodied shoeprints were Keene's and showed that he was bleeding profusely while attempting to flee from his attacker or attackers. Watson believed the wounds to the neck and back were made after Keene was either on the ground or in pursuit.

John Kelso. *From the* Erie Daily Times.

Hanley remarked that he believed the weapon used was likely a corn-cutter, which prompted a response from Detective Watson.

"When you see the weapon you will not think it was a corn knife."[63]

The jury continued questioning Watson, asking if the weapon had been found. Watson refused to answer, and Hanley interjected that an answer was not recommended in terms of the murder weapon. The coroner's jury returned a verdict: "Death resulted from wounds inflicted upon him by a sharp instrument in the hands of a party or parties unknown to the jury."[64]

Following the inquiry, Watson's investigation steered him to the Algeria Stock Farm, owned by former Erie mayor and representative William L. Scott. Watson received a tip from W.P. Anderson, who had been training a trotting horse that Scott owned. Anderson told Watson he may have been a witness to strange events possibly connected to Keene's murder.

Anderson exited the Waldameer trolley at 9:00 p.m., getting off at the Algeria Farm. Arriving at the farmhouse, he retired to his room, which looked out onto West Lake Road. Hearing loud voices, Anderson looked out the window and saw the shapes of what appeared to be four or five men talking loudly. After what appeared to be a heated discussion, one of the men started walking away, heading in the direction of the Kelso farm, leaving the rest of the group in the middle of the road. Recording Anderson's story, Watson then inspected other areas of the farm before heading back to Erie.

Keene's murder had John Kelso and his family on edge. Albert Kelso's son, Harry, stayed at John Kelso's house, going to bed with a shotgun for protection. Anna Kelso, John's daughter-in-law, had gone into Erie to stay with the Keene family. And the night before the funeral, John Keene ventured to the Albert Kelso residence, with both men performing a thorough search of the property before they started to drain the large duck pond behind Albert's house, attempting to locate the murder weapon.

Within a day, the pond was drained, and a careful search was made of the muddy bottom. It failed to reveal the murder weapon.

On the morning of October 26, 1909, Keene's body was laid out at his residence. The services were largely attended by friends and relatives along with a delegation from the Carpenters Union. The *Erie Daily Times* reported that the "usual morbid crowd"[65] present on such occasions was noticeably absent. Following the services, the body was removed to St. Patrick's Church, where a requiem High Mass was performed by Father Joseph Cauley. Before the services ended, Cauley spoke about Keene's murderer: "As for the one that has committed this crime, if there is one who regrets the deed, it is he. It is an awful thing to have the thought of murder in the heart."[66]

WHO DID IT?

Editorial cartoon drawn by *Erie Daily Times* cartoonist Walter Kiedaisch. *From the* Erie Daily Times.

Following the services, Keene's body was transported to Trinity Cemetery and interred in a grave near where Detective Sergeant James Higgins was buried in 1905. The morbid onlookers who were absent at the Keene residence clung to the iron gates of the cemetery, the men present removing their hats as others burst into tears once the casket was lowered into the earth.

On West Lake road, traffic continued as usual. The bloodstains were still present at the scene, greeting onlookers who visited the spot. Several days later, the *Erie Dispatch* reported: "Automobiles halted, carriages stopped, while their curious occupants drew and hushed the throbbing motors to hear the crying of the blood from the ground."[67]

Reporters also called at the Erie County Jail, asking if any arrests had been made, only to be told County Detective Watson was not in his office. They then flocked to the occupants of West Lake Road questioning anyone they could come across, only to find that those in the countryside had not seen Detective Watson either.

"He didn't stop this way,"[68] replied one of the farmers.

Five days had eclipsed since Manley Keene's mangled body was found on West Lake Road, and the press fixed the blame on Frank Watson for his inability to "fix" the crime on the responsible person or persons. Rumors continued in the streets, alleyways and smoke-filled saloons of Erie and its nearby towns and boroughs. Perhaps an arrest was close at hand? Speculation spread like wildfire. Some believed Keene was a victim of mistaken identity, others suicide. Such theories were investigated early on and had been widely discredited.

Other rumors were more credible, such as a persistent belief there were problems between the Keene and Kelso families, causing members of both families to become besieged by a sea of reporters and detectives on a daily basis. The stress reached such a point that John Kelso's aged sister remarked to a reporter for the *Times* on October 27 that she was worried the public suspected someone within her family as being the murderer.

As for the *Erie Dispatch*, the paper issued a blistering response to what it saw as a lack of cooperation between city and county authorities, stating:

> *The county commissioners have done all in their power to attain the ends of justice. It now remains for the detectives and police to show their skill. Even though it is a bit hard to have to exert oneself, particular when well paid for sticking to one beat, still a thousand dollars is not to be sneezed at and we hope for results—now.*[69]

In response to the growing pressure in the case, on October 27, Chief of Police Edward Wagner detailed Detective Sergeant John Welsh of the Erie City Police Department to the Keene case along with County Detective Watson. Following a meeting with Chief Wagner that night, Detective Welsh left the station in search of clues, working into the early morning hours of the twenty-eighth.

Detective Sergeant John Esmond Welsh was born in Waterford, Ireland, and had immigrated to the United States, settling in Erie. Welsh joined the police department in 1897, rose through the ranks from patrolman to detective sergeant and was

Detective Sergeant John E. Welsh. *Author's collection.*

46

well regarded within the department. Wagner hoped that assigning Welsh to the Keene murder would provide Detective Watson with much-needed assistance in bringing Keene's murderer to justice.

The case would soon take another turn, adding another bizarre angle to the already mysterious murder case.

Mysteries Persist, Theories Abound

On October 18, 1909, the *Erie Daily Times* unveiled what it believed was a major breakthrough in the case, a clue that pointed to motive for murder. At the time of his death, Keene possessed a total of $15,000 in life insurance policies that had been taken out in his name. The *Times* claimed that Keene was worth more dead than alive and reported that a suspect, a relative of Keene's, had financial issues prior to Keene's murder. These clues, the *Times* claimed, went ignored by the police.

The *Times* laid out in extensive detail the separate life insurance policies, pointing to them as the motive for the murder. What it also did was dig deep into the personal lives of Keene's family members, exposing personal details to the public when the paper claimed that Keene was "physically incompetent," adding that his daughters were adopted and his son, John, was Leona's son from a prior marriage.

The *Times* proceeded to lay out its case for who murdered Manley Keene, evidence that was also purportedly supported by a report claiming John and Leona Keene were submitted to "sweating"[70] before Chief Wagner and Detective Welsh.

John Keene directed a response to the *Times*:

> *We were willing to do this and we walked up to the station, Detective Welsh walking slightly ahead of us. We had not thought of being sweated, and while in the chief's office nothing of the kind occurred. We simply gave the police department such information in regard to Mr. Keene, as was in our power to do.*[71]

Reaction to the *Times* was swift and negative. Detective Welsh and Chief Wagner released statements, insisting that John and Leona Keene were merely questioned about several items of concern in the investigation and allowed to leave. While it was clear that the *Times* was attempting to reach deep into Keene's family in search of clues that would point to Keene's murder, the results were viewed as having gone too far.

The *Erie Dispatch* took a reduced role in reporting the news about Keene's life insurance policies, noting that the policies were taken out after Keene's almost fatal injury and that the policies were taken out more so for financial security for Keene's wife and children because of his diminished health. The *Dispatch*'s view of the questioning of John and Leona Keene also disputed that any sweating had occurred.

A more interesting piece of information, provided by the *Dispatch*, revealed that Keene's will had been revised on September 6, 1909. After the revision, the will left his entire estate to his wife with the additional authority passed onto his children if something should happen to Leona. The *Dispatch*'s response to the *Times* also revealed the rivalry between the two papers, with the *Dispatch* claiming that it was the only newspaper in Erie with "sufficient enterprise"[72] to present the facts of the case as soon as they developed.

It was clear that both newspapers in Erie were on a quest to sensationalize the story and sell more papers, all this of course happening with no new developments in the investigation. While the papers battled each other in a series of exchanges on the morning of the twenty-eighth, Chief of Police Wagner met at City Hall with Detectives Wagner and Watson to discuss the case behind closed doors. When Watson arrived at 10:00 a.m., a crowd of reporters was waiting for him, and he refused to issue a statement.

When Watson exited the conference into the hallway of city hall, he continued his vow of silence as he made his way back to his office at the Erie County Courthouse. Another cursory search had been performed at the Kelso farms along with additional searches in the city in an attempt to locate the weapon—leaving authorities coming back empty-handed again.

The *Times* was in damage control mode and acknowledged that gossip and theories did not constitute evidence:

> *Just because a man may have had personal differences with his wife or children, adopted or otherwise, is no good reason for believing they would take his life in the most deliberate and dastardly manner. Just because a man carried a little more life insurance than one in his position in life perhaps could well afford to carry, while possibly under certain circumstances might be forged into a connecting link to complete a chain, would fall far short of making the chain itself.[73]*

At a perilous moment in the investigation into the murder of Manley Keene, the *Times*'s next gamble was a financial investment that sought to bring Keene's murderer to justice. It was a move that would not only forever change the Erie City Police Department and its handling of investigations but also herald the arrival of the "Female Sherlock Holmes": private detective Mary E. Holland.

A FAMOUS DETECTIVE JOINS THE CASE

On October 29, 1909, a female private detective stepped off a train from Chicago, Illinois, as it sat at the platform of Erie's Union Depot. At forty-one years old, Mary Holland was regarded as the world's most famous female detective. Her reputation as the "Female Sherlock Holmes" preceded her in an age when women still were not afforded the same liberties as men. She had worked and trained with Scotland Yard in London; assisted authorities in Paris, France; and worked with over a dozen police departments throughout the United States. Holland also established the Identification Bureau of the Naval Department at Washington.[74]

Private detective Mary E. Holland. *By Gary Dombrowski.*

A student of noted French police officer Alphonse Bertillion, Holland was also the American agent for the Bertillion system and helped train local departments to use the identification system.[75] By 1909, most departments, including Erie, had made extensive use of the fingerprint and Bertillion systems due in part to Holland's work.

"There is no work a man does that a woman cannot do just as well," Holland said in 1908. "My belief in my sex, its brain and ability is strong and deep-rooted."[76]

Along with Holland's arrival, Erie saw an immediate influx of lesser-known private detectives and sleuths who had been attracted to the handsome reward offer of $1,000 to apprehend Keene's murderer. Holland's track record of working with police and securing convictions was seen as a welcome addition to the investigation, and city officials initially welcomed her with open arms.

"It's a great newspaper stunt, it certainly shows enterprise,"[77] remarked Erie County district attorney William Pitt Gifford. Chief Wagner, too, went on to say there was enough room for everyone to join the investigation. Both men said they stood ready to assist Holland in any way possible. Police captain John P. Sullivan proclaimed, "It is a master stroke, and without doubt the biggest stunt ever pulled off by an Erie newspaper."[78]

While public officials commented extensively on the *Times*'s decision to involve Mary Holland in the Keene murder investigation, any mention of this was virtually nonexistent in the pages of the *Erie Dispatch*. In fact, the *Dispatch* proclaimed that at that point city and county authorities were working in harmony and believed an arrest to be imminent.

Additional conferences occurred between Chief Wagner and Detectives Walsh and Watson, and the detectives were working nonstop. They attempted to keep their movements as discreet as possible. When Mary Holland joined the sensationalized hunt for Keene's killer, the police's attention had returned to the blood found on John Kelso's veranda, in an attempt to analyze the best evidence they possessed.

When Holland began her search for Manley Keene's killer, she hit the ground running, venturing out into Millcreek Township, questioning those who lived in the vicinity of the murder. The Burger sisters, who resided in a small country home nestled among trees and flowers on West Lake Road, told Holland that on the day before Keene's body was found, they passed John Kelso's residence. They thought they saw Kelso's son Edwin often referred to as "Crazy" Kelso.[79] Holland noted that Edwin Kelso was institutionalized at Warren State Hospital but suggested he might have escaped.

Holland believed the sighting of Edwin Kelso might not mean anything, and in response, the *Times* sent two reporters to Warren to check on Kelso. Holland also added that there were families on West Eighth Street who claimed a strange man prowled the neighborhoods in the early hours, ringing bells and creating a disturbance.

Unbeknownst to Mary Holland, Edwin Kelso had already been eliminated by County Detective Watson. In the beginning stages of the investigation Watson confirmed that Kelso was still safely tucked away at Warren State Hospital. The *Dispatch* dissected the Burger sisters statements and, in a tongue-and-cheek response to its competitor, said, "The alleged 'clew' of the *Erie Daily Times*, regarding the possible connection of Edwin Kelso with the murder of Manla [sic] W. Keene, has fallen flat."[80]

It was also known that Charles Raymond, Keene's brother-in-law, was at Warren State Hospital. A detective working on the case suggested "the

Mary Holland inspecting the location by the walnut tree where Manley Keene was attacked. *From the* Erie Daily Times.

Mary Holland, Hugh C. Weir and *Times* editor George Reid Yaple examine where Keene's body was found. Note the bloodstains. *From the* Erie Daily Times.

Times may be reserving this for another sensational cock and bull story."[81] In articles for the *Times*, Holland suggested that all theories must be discarded and the investigation revisited from a fresh angle. Upon reviewing the known evidence at that point, Holland deduced that none of the theories on motive was ever closely analyzed.

"When I arrived in this city yesterday, there seemed a wealth of clues and theories," Holland wrote. "In fact, there seemed too many. It was much like a maze where you didn't know which way to turn." In reference to the theories, Holland said, "None of them has borne—can bear—a close inspection."[82]

Holland also gave her opinion about Keene's death:

I am convinced that the first blow was that which entered the upper portion of the left man's arm. The assassin might have been crouching for his victim by the side of the path and struck at his heart, the knife instead entering his arm. The second blow struck his arm at a lower point. The third blow was that which killed him—not the gash in his throat, but the downward sweeping blow, which severed the big artery of his leg. It was this wound that killed him. Now we are to infer that, not satisfied with his work, the assassin pursued Keene as he ran, striking blow after blow into his back, and finally, just as he was falling in a dying condition from the loss of blood, caught him by the collar and severed the jugular vein of his throat.[83]

Holland referenced other strange facts within the case. Keene had not visited the Kelso farm for six months, and on his last visit, few knew he was there. "Why should any stranger expect Keene to be there the night of the murder if he was not a constant visitor to the farm?" Holland asked.

If Keene was attacked by a stranger, why did he not run back to the Kelso residence for aid? If he was attacked at the front of the Kelso residence, why not run back inside? It was also odd that John Kelso and his daughter-in-law had stated that Keene's reason for not staying was his wife would be worried if he had not returned home. It was common knowledge the Keene family had a Bell telephone. John's cousin Albert Kelso also had a telephone. Keene could have simply telephoned his wife, telling her that he would be staying with the Kelsos. Why did he insist on leaving?

Keene's insurance policies were not regarded as suspicious, according to Holland. Believing that there were those in the vicinity of West Lake Road who had not come forward, Holland made an impassioned plea: "It seems to me that every person living near the vicinity of the Kelso home should come forward in a spirit of public duty."

Mary Holland inspects the door frame of the John Kelso residence. *Author's collection.*

By this point in the investigation, police had cleared Keene's son, John, of any involvement in the murder. Keene was observed at his residence in Erie around 10:00 p.m. and was seen by several individuals. Streetcar crews who ventured out to Waldameer were also questioned, and their testimonies failed to shed any light on suspicious-looking passengers. Holland's arrival in Erie provided a spark that threw the investigation into overdrive and kept the morbidly curious involved with daily updates in the case. Onlookers still crowded around the murder scene and outside John Kelso's residence.

On November 1, reporters from the *Times* had been shadowing individuals around both Kelso farms and reported that around 2:30 p.m. a police dragnet had been placed about the house. Detective Welsh appeared on the scene and crept into the Kelso Barn. Soon he was joined by Chief Wagner and Detective Watson. Holland, who was near the scene, had asked for assistance from the police in arresting an individual to bring them into the city. Holland's request was denied, with police advising they were not sure her request was entirely within their legal authority.

"It was handled in the yellowest Sunday magazine style somewhat in accord with the Wellington-Blucher meeting after the victory of Waterloo,"[84] mocked the *Erie Dispatch*, in response to what appeared to be another embarrassing false alarm by the *Times*. The *Dispatch* remarked the dragnet was nothing more than a gathering of authorities for a quick meeting.

A Maze of Theories and Endless Suspects

Mary Holland received a letter on November 1 from a female clairvoyant in Northeast claiming that Keene had been murdered by a farmhand who attacked him in a case of mistaken identity. This was supported, according to the clairvoyant, by a love triangle gone wrong. The murderer, she claimed, was long gone, having already traveled west. Other strange incidents brought to Holland's attention involved a mud-covered carriage that thundered along West Lake Road on the night of October 22, its two male occupants appearing suspicious when spotted in Erie.

The evidence before Mary Holland presented more questions than answers, the most troubling being no autopsy was performed on Keene's body. According to Holland, if the murderer was ever apprehended, the absence of an autopsy would make prosecution more difficult. In reviewing the details surrounding Keene's wounds, Holland claimed the stab wound in Keene's chest not only went through the body but also appeared to have entered in the front—not the back. Strangely, this wound did not cut the fabric of the coat or vest.

Holland incorrectly noted that Keene's clothing showed no signs of distress: the vest certainly showed signs of a struggle, with the buttons torn away and not recovered. Keene's shirt was also torn, and he possessed defensive wounds.

"Was Keene murdered where he was found?" Holland asked hypothetically. There was the strange way in which Keene was found that morning, with his overcoat buttoned over his clothes—and the knife marks in his trunk—and his hat also still on his head. Holland still said she could not rule out the possibility that Keene had been murdered elsewhere and transported to West Lake Road.

It was during this time that the buttons from Keene's vest were suddenly located near where Keene's body had been found. After over a dozen intensive searches in the area, had the buttons been overlooked? Or, more importantly, had Keene's killer discarded the buttons, feeling the heat of the investigation was so much that he needed to get rid of the evidence? Holland, assisted by two men, had also searched that area thoroughly and not located anything.

Public sentiment in response to the failure of an autopsy continued to grow, with one prominent citizen, who declined to be named, stating, "I am surprised that anyone would think of burying the body, under the conditions, without everything being done in the way of a post mortem. The people should now demand that this be done before it is too late."[85]

On the morning of November 6, 1909, the intrusion into the lives of the Keene and Kelso families reached a boiling point. Through their attorneys, the families issued a statement to the public:

> *The privacy of our homes has been invaded by persons unauthorized to do so, and unannounced, and we have endured all this for such a length of time that we now feel that we have some rights which even self-appointed or hired detectives are bound to respect. From this time on we will not permit our premises to be invaded or ourselves molested by any so-called detectives, either self-appointed or hired for sensational other purposes, and hereby notify them all not to interfere with us or enter upon our premises.* [86]

It is clear the Keene and Kelso families were taking issue with the *Times* and the paper bringing Mary Holland into the case. Frederick S. Phelps, editor for the *Erie Daily Times*, responded defiantly, "The *Times* is a newspaper, run in the interests of the public and is not going to be switched off the track one way or another."[87]

With the families taking a firm stance against Holland's investigation, along with the absence of cooperation from local authorities, Mary Holland was forced to continue through other means. She reviewed, again, the evidence. Again, she also requested assistance from the public: "There must be other persons, who passed along the road, either during the night or the early morning. Saturday was market morning, and the traffic must have been fairly heavy. If you can help me, I will appreciate your assistance."[88]

Holland's other appeal, to the district attorney, along with the growing resentment over the absence of an autopsy, also went unanswered. District Attorney Gifford told the *Times* there was no evidence that supported the exhumation and criticized the *Times* stating that the recent reporting was unsubstantiated, imaginative and "yellow in nature."[89]

Erie County District Attorney William Pitt Gifford. *From the* Erie Daily Times.

THE MADMAN OF WEST LAKE ROAD

Detective Welsh returned to the crime scene on November 7, 1909, spending a considerable time in the neighboring area. At this point in the investigation, Detective Watson was inundated with additional work while preparing for the opening of the November term of Quarter Sessions Court, requiring his presence at the Erie County Courthouse.

The murder, still the main topic of gossip in Erie, was coupled with the fact that it was known the investigation had appeared to reach a dead end, not only for city and county authorities but for Mary Holland as well. This was clear with the articles that appeared in the *Times* over the days that followed, defensive in nature as far as justifying Holland's presence still in Erie and the investigation.

Additional theories made their way into the pages of the press. A madman waving a knife had attacked an Erie grocer and his wife on West Lake Road. An insane mane was seen on Waldameer Beach shortly before the murder. Holland had revisited several items located around the murder, such as the hickory club, which had already been discounted. Holland's attention turned to the knife-wielding madman of West Lake Road.

"I am convinced that he must have been a smart crazy man to think of so much, especially to throw blood on a nearby veranda to mislead the detectives," wrote a local citizen in an editorial to the *Times*.

After being rebuked by the district attorney, Holland turned to the rumor that Keene had a wound on his forehead. This, she wrote later, was an additional piece of evidence that warranted Keene's exhumation—to put any false stories and gossip to rest. Holland also accused County Detective Watson of not wanting to take the hickory club into his possession.

The sensationalized investigation of Mary Holland came to a halt when she was called back to Chicago on the night of November 11, 1909. The *Times* assured its readers that Holland was not abandoning the case and took the opportunity to criticize the city and county authorities: "It is safe to say that had the police and county authorities been co-operating with Mrs. Holland, her evidence before this would have been placed at their disposal and an arrest in the case undoubtedly would have been made several days ago."[90]

The *Erie Dispatch*, surprisingly, issued a more scathing rebuke of the police in reference to increased criminal activity: "Something is radically wrong in the police department. Erie is paying its policemen a fair wage and they have had the nerve to ask for an increase from councils on top

THE MYSTERY PLANT

Editorial cartoon drawn by cartoonist Walter Kiedaisch. *From the* Erie Daily Times.

of this evidence of their utter unfitness for the positions they hold."[91] In criticizing the police for unsolved murders in Erie that year, the *Dispatch* continued, "Ten burglaries in 20 days and property loss exceeding $3,000 is a dark record for a city which claims to be progressive and up to date. It is a record which no live city should stand for week in and week out with some good and sufficient reason."[92]

RENEWED VIGOR AND HOPELESS THOUGHTS

The Keene murder still generated headlines during Mary Holland's absence. For instance, a bloody dollar bill was found by David Swanson on West Lake Road. While working on the Kelso farm, Swanson kicked up the dollar bill from the leaves of the gutter next to the footpath where Keene had been found. Just the day prior, Swanson claimed he had found a dime in the same area. The *Times*, of course, jumped on this as potential evidence and asked if it, too, had a role to play in the murder. The money, along with an additional report of a supposed lunatic sharpening a knife at the Erie County Almshouse, did not pan out and neither appears to have been involved in the murder.

When Mary Holland returned from Chicago on November 17, she set out to analyze the bloodstained dollar bill. At this point in the investigation, for reasons that remain a mystery, Detectives Watson and Welsh set out for Buffalo to investigation potential leads there.

There was also additional excitement when authorities in the nearby village of Greenville arrested a possible suspect. A detective for the Bessemer Railroad spotted a suspicious individual, and a brief pursuit culminated in a brawl before the man was arrested, giving his name as Frank Hanna of Niles, Ohio. Detective Welsh traveled to Greenville, examined Hanna and concluded he was not involved in the murder.

And just as news had been reported of the authorities' trip to Buffalo, Holland announced her investigation had stretched to Buffalo as well as Chicago and even New Orleans; however, these "clues" appeared to relate more to Keene's business relationships with individuals in other cities.

The *Times* responded to mocking by the *Dispatch* by claiming, "The efforts of the Tenth street sheet to cover up the fact that it never does anything worthwhile in the way of giving its readers the real facts in a big case like the Keene murder mystery, are laughable."[93] When the *Dispatch* discounted the bloody dollar bill and almshouse lunatic sighting as having no significance in the case, the *Times* continued its rebuttal: "If all statements made by The Tenth street sheet are as completely false as that one, then the fact that practically no one reads the old rag is easily understood."[94]

Mary Holland was left grasping at straws. The Keene and Kelso families had refused to further cooperate with private investigators and sleuths from the city. The district attorney forbade the exhumation of Keene's body. There was tremendous strain between the private detective and local authorities. Holland, who prided herself on working in conjunction with local police departments, came to the realization that such would not occur in Erie. By November 20, Holland had run out of avenues and, instead, turned her attention to writing an article that focused on modern approved methods that were being instituted by departments throughout the country and how such revitalization could improve Erie's police department.

The restructuring needed in Erie's police department, according to Holland, pointed a finger directly at Chief of Police Edward Wagner. A chief of police, claimed Holland, should not be appointed for political gain and should be someone who has made crime detection his life's work.[95]

Local authorities in Erie had the opportunity to better themselves for future investigations. Whether they would take heed of Holland's suggestions, however, remained to be seen.

Time of Reflection and Lessons Learned

The Erie Police Department was put to the test on November 25, 1909, when forty-five-year-old Vincenzo Monacello was shot and killed at the corner of West Fourth and Plum Streets by Alessandro Di Bello. The shooting triggered an immediate manhunt for Di Bello and an all hands on deck approach from County Detective Watson, who helped assist. The *Times* commended the police for the quick and thorough work[96] in the search for Di Bello and praised Captain William Detzel for his quick thinking and organization of the investigation. Di Bello ultimately evaded detection and prosecution and was never located; he escaped, presumably, to the security of his family in Philadelphia.

The last significant developments of the Manley Keene investigation appeared on November 27, when a pair of eyeglasses were found on West Lake Road. The glasses, which were intact, were enclosed in a case with an inscription, "C.C. French," listed on the inside. It was later determined the glasses, constructed in a unique way, were made by local optician Clarence C. French and prescribed for Manley Keene. More puzzling was that the police were unaware that Keene possessed a second pair of glasses, something not revealed by his family.

At about the same time the discovery of Keene's glasses hit the front pages, Mary Holland appears to have quietly left Erie, leaving the search for Keene's killer in the hands of local authorities and a handful of amateur sleuths and private detectives in the city. After Holland's departure, the criticism of the police again hit a fever pitch in a blistering editorial after the arrest of Eugene Tallman in the shooting death of John May in Girard:

> *The police and the county detective combined have not so much as been able to make an arrest. Comment is hardly necessary, unless it be to the effect*

Sketch of Manla Keene's glasses found some distance from scene of murder by Times representatives.

Keene's glasses, which were found some considerable time after the murder. Drawn by cartoonist Walter Kiedaisch. *From the* Erie Daily Times.

that it might not be a bad idea to import some of the county constables to Erie for police duty and detective work. They seem to know how to turn the tricks, while our city officers and county detective do not.[97]

The *Times* continued its criticism of Watson:

If Detective Watson has given up the chase for the Keene murderer, let the county commissioners insist on bringing in two or three competent detectives into the case and they will not be very long in securing the assassin. To give up the work simply because the detectives is unable to land the offender or offenders is no reason whatever why Erie county should permit criminals to escape.[98]

In the end, the Keene investigation—although flawed and at times improperly executed—did bring much-needed changes to the department. Although the search for Vincenzo Monacello's murderer failed to bring about an arrest, it showed the city's police capable of adapting to an ever-changing world in investigations.

Until his death in 1921 at the age of sixty-four, Frank H. Watson remained the county detective in Erie. Following the Keene investigation, the improved cooperation between county and city officials were clearly on display in the

1920 investigation into the murder of Austrian immigrant Szima Florian. Watson's work and cooperation in the case helped find evidence that secured the death penalty for Florian's four killers[99]—a first in Pennsylvania history.

County Detective Watson was also an unnoted victim in the Keene murder. Investigators back then did not have the luxury of those today in the realm of technology and advanced forensics. Watson was also working as the sole county detective, and he was often burdened with a heavy workload. At the time, cooperation between county and local officials was more relaxed and uncommon. Today, 145 years after the county detective position was established by the Erie County District Attorney's Office, Erie County employs nine detectives. They are often asked to assist in investigations that occur beyond the jurisdictions of certain departments. The Erie County Detectives Office also helps manage task forces to reduce elder abuse, cyber crime, DUI, child abuse, major crimes and criminal investigations, including drug interdiction and domestic violence.

The absence of an autopsy of Manley Keene plagued the Erie County coroner in the following elections, and from that moment on, autopsies would be performed on murder investigations within Erie County. It would not be until January 1983, however, that a forensic pathologist would be involved in an autopsy in Erie County—during the investigation into the homicide of Frank "Bolo" Dovishaw.

Toward the end of 1909, Leona Keene received $3,000 from one of the life insurances her husband took out. Leona died in 1934 at the age of seventy-one while visiting her daughter in Naples, New York. Her son, John, died in 1926, when he succumbed to a brain tumor that caused an auto accident. They are both interred in the Keene family plot in Trinity Cemetery, just a few minutes' walk from where Keene met his gruesome end.

As a heavy snow fell on the city of Erie and 1910 began, Detective Sergeant Welsh was removed from the Keene case and returned to regular duty. The department continued to be plagued with criticism throughout the remainder of Chief of Police Wagner's tenure. This continued until December 4, 1911, when William F. Detzel was promoted to chief of police by newly elected mayor William J. Stern. Detzel's appointment to the head of Erie's police department would see an overall improvement in criminal investigations, although Erie would continue to be notorious—and always had—for its attraction to criminals from all walks of life.

Despite some of the immediate changes to the Erie Police Department following the Manley Keene investigation, the department faced challenges that hindered its criminal investigations for years to come. It wasn't until

Above: Present-day photograph of West Lake Road where Manley Keene was murdered. *Author's collection.*

Left: Grave of Manley W. Keene. *Author's collection.*

the 1920s that the department added a Bertillion department to help aid investigators and detectives.

Mary E. Holland never returned to Erie, and the Manley Keene murder faded into obscurity—where it has remained ever since. Holland gained greater fame in the 1910 murder trial of Thomas Jennings in Chicago, when she was called on as a fingerprint expert. Due in part to Holland's testimony, Jennings was found guilty of shooting Clarence Hiller. It was the first criminal trial to use evidence of fingerprint analysis. Jennings would be executed in 1912. Holland would continue to assist departments from her detective agency and further assisted the Chicago Police Department until her death on March 27, 1915, after contracting pneumonia following surgery. She was just forty-seven years old.

The location on West Lake Road where Manley Keene was mutilated still exists, although the once vibrant farm fields and houses have been replaced with urbanization and residential streets. The intersection with Orange Avenue, next to Presque Isle Skating, is where Keene's body was located. Both of the Kelso farms are long gone; however, local roads still bear connection to Erie's history. This is clear with the nearby Kelso Beach Drive, which is where Albert Kelso's farm used to be. Just as it was in 1909, West Lake Road remains a busy thoroughfare in Millcreek Township, used by tourists who visit Waldameer and Presque Isle. The old chestnut tree that witnessed Manley Keene's death stood undisturbed well into the 1960s, rumored among local teenage thrill seekers to be haunted.

Keeping vigil overlooking Manley Keene's grave in Trinity Cemetery is a six-foot-tall statue capped with a kneeling angel. It was erected in April 1910 and designed by the Union Monument Works. The angel is still there, keeping an everlasting vigil over the Keene family.

3

A CAMPAIGN OF TERROR

The Pennsylvania Railroad Coal Trestle Bombing

In the early morning hours of January 29, 1911, a brittle wind blew against the black hulls of ships docked in the middle of Presque Isle Bay. Larger freighters sat moored to the docks, water sloshing against the steel and shoreline next to an endless maze of railroad tracks and warehouses.

All was quiet. That is, until 1:15 a.m., when the bayfront was rocked by a massive explosion from the mass of steel that was the Pennsylvania Railroad Coal Trestle. The shock wave, felt throughout the entire First Ward, smashed windows and rattled houses.[100] Families exited the warm confines of their homes while others shrugged it off, thinking it was the dropping of slag near the Perry Iron Works.

By 2:30 a.m., police headquarters had become inundated with phone calls reporting the explosion. Captain William F. Detzel sprang into action along with Detective Sergeant John Grant and a handful of men and headed to the docks.

Police arrived at the Pennsylvania Railroad Coal Trestle and were greeted with a smoldering mass of twisted steel, splintered wood and debris strewn all over. One of the large steel girders had struck the *Mary C. Elpiske*, a coal boat moored alongside the trestle;[101] the force was so incredible that despite weighing 1,200 pounds the girder was thrown 600 feet away. The cement northeastern portion of the trestle was shattered by the blast.[102]

Incredibly, the explosion caused no fatalities. While rummaging through the wreckage, police learned Watchman Patrick Cribbins had been nearby when it happened. Following the explosion, Cribbins immediately arrived at the scene but was unable to locate those responsible.

The Pennsylvania Railroad Coal Trestle at the Anchor Line Docks. *Library of Congress.*

SCENE OF SUNDAY MORNING'S EXPLOSION AT COAL DOCKS

Showing the wrecked trestle, and the damage done when the bomb was set off early Sunday morning. The explosive was placed at the southeast end of the trestle.

Photograph showing the destruction caused by the explosion to the Pennsylvania Railroad Coal Trestle. *From the* Erie Daily Times.

The early hours of the morning saw Detective Sergeant John Welsh assigned to work on the case. It was revealed that the bomb had been placed under the eastern side of the trestle, directly under one of the large steel uprights, likely done with the perpetrators standing on a float while fixing the explosives to the steel frame. Police also located evidence the watchman's shanty had been broken into on the night of the twenty-eighth. Evidence inside the shanty led police to believe those responsible prepared the bombs and then fixed the wiring to detonate the charges, although they were still unsure whether dynamite or nitroglycerine was used.

The bombers miscalculated the placement of the bomb. Had it been placed on the additional dock upright, on the other side, it is likely the entire steel trestle would've destroyed the *Mary C. Elpiske*, certainly causing fatalities. Erie City Police were joined by authorities from Cleveland and the Pennsylvania Railroad Police, with Chief of Police Wagner offering every form of assistance available.

It was not long before they discovered a motive.

A DEADLY MOTIVE

America was a rapidly changing country in 1911. Technology was improving, and Americans were moving on to bigger and better things. Erie's population was steadily increasing, and the numerous docks and fisheries along Erie's bayfront continued to provide a steady supply of employment. Although prosperous, 1911 also showed troubling signs with the onset of strikes at manufacturing plants throughout the country and the growing power of labor unions. By 1910, for example, U.S. Steel had succeeded in removing all unions from its plants. Further anti-union sentiment spread throughout the country, and in return, union officials resorted to violence in retaliation.

The bombing of the coal trestle in Erie was not isolated, either. Both before and after the bombing there were a reported one hundred bridges and iron-related structures wrecked or bombed by "unknown miscreants."[103] Bombings in the neighboring state of Ohio were said to be specifically "union-related."

When questioned by a reporter from the *Times*, an official with the Pennsylvania Railroad remarked, "Has it come to pass, that people must put uniformed guards about their property and arm them with Winchester

Rifles? Human life is sacred, but property must be protected. There are places where we can ship coal without being interfered with and if necessary we can fold our tent and go elsewhere."[104]

While the trestle was out of operation, the Pennsylvania Railroad was suffering. Time was money.

"What will [*sic*] happen if another explosion occurred?" inquired the reporter.

"Let me tell you; they had better not try it, that is all!"[105] responded the official, slamming his fist against the table.

MYSTERIES ABOUND A WELL-LAID PLOT

At the time of its construction, the Pennsylvania Railroad Coal Trestle was being leased by the Susquehanna Coal Company, with the original contract handled by the McMyler Manufacturing Company of Cleveland, Ohio, for producing the steel girders. There was, however, pressure from the Susquehanna Coal Company to rush production in time to have operations beginning on March 1.

This sudden change in plans meant a subcontract was involved, utilizing the J.F. McCain Construction Company of Mercer, Pennsylvania, which would then oversee the remainder of the construction. The McCain Construction Company, however, was also reportedly not on good terms with the union. This became apparent when two prior bridge projects involving the McCain Construction Company were targeted by dynamiters, one of them in Buffalo.

Spectators curiously gawked at the wreckage while police continued the investigation with every officer who could be spared. Meanwhile, an additional search of the wreckage located a second can of high explosives. Authorities concluded the explosive was not manufactured in Erie and had been brought from somewhere else. The can filled with nitroglycerine, complete with a fuse, was turned over to Cleveland authorities. In examining the can to determine why it failed to ignite, police learned it was due to a poor job of splicing the fuse. With the evidence police had uncovered, they believed the length of the fuse allowed the bombers at least twenty minutes to escape.

Hope that the perpetrators would be apprehended was quickly squashed, as police suspected those responsible were already hundreds of miles away. In the days that followed, local railroad detectives remained on high alert

Advertisement appearing in the newspaper purporting to show a sketch of what the explosive looked like. *From the* Erie Daily Times.

and had increased patrols. On February 1, 1911, six men acting suspiciously near the wreckage were arrested and charged with trespassing.[106]

Pennsylvania Railroad officials approached the Erie City Police Department to inquire about providing temporary assistance to guard the trestle from further attacks. Officials were left irritated when the department advised that because they would not be paid they could not guard railroad property. This was in stark contrast to when the police guarded and protected the Scott Mausoleum—it was desecrated a day prior—causing backlash in the press.[107]

The investigation quickly went cold, at least in the eyes of the public. Several weeks later, mysterious advertisements appeared in the *Times*. The advertisement, accompanied by a photograph of the second can of explosives, offered a $500 reward for information. The address for the communication, treated confidentially, was said to be traced to authorities in Cleveland, Ohio.

Police were soon provided with the possible identities of those responsible for the bombing, all thanks to famed private detective William J. Burns.

A CAMPAIGN OF UNIONIZED TERROR

On April 22, 1911, private detective William J. Burns arrived at the headquarters of the Iron Workers Union in Indianapolis, Indiana. Entering the executive board meeting, Burns arrested the secretary treasurer, John J. McNamara. Only days before, McNamara's brother James and Ortie McManigal were arrested at the Oxford Hotel in Detroit, Michigan. The three men were immediately shuttled to Los Angeles and charged with the bombing of the Los Angeles Times Building on October 1, 1910.

During the early morning hours of October 1, 1910, at the *Los Angeles Times*'s office, employees were working late to prepare an extra edition for the paper. A suitcase filled with sixteen sticks of dynamite had been left in a narrow alley between the Times building and an annex known as "Ink

Alley." At 1:07 a.m., it exploded, igniting a natural gas pipeline in the building and creating a massive explosion, killing twenty-one people. News of the explosion traveled around the world.

Los Angeles mayor George Alexander hired William J. Burns, the famous private detective, the following day. At the time, Burns had already been working on an investigation on behalf of the National Erectors' Association involving the Iron Manufacture Plant bombings, which occurred the previous year. Through a various array of informants and spies, Burns homed in on the McNamara brothers and McManigal and wove a web of evidence against them.

Several months after the Los Angeles Times Bombing, the Iron Workers Union had again plotted another series of bombings, set to go off on December 25. The bombing campaign of terror failed with McManigal, who did not succeed in damaging the Llewellyn Iron Works and abandoned the additional bombings.

The arrest of the officials of the International Union of Bridge and Structural Workers gave Erie police an indication that it was likely tied to the trestle bombing. It had been noted that cans and blasting caps confiscated by Burns and his detective agency were strikingly similar to the second can located at the coal trestle, although some minor differences between both bombings existed.[108]

The arrest of the McNamara brothers set off a nationwide outrage against the national labor movement, which felt that the brothers were being unfairly imprisoned and treated and attempted to spin it as a conspiracy led by William J. Burns. The Iron Workers Union rallied behind the McNamaras, who received an additional boost when it was announced they would be represented by famed defense attorney Clarence Darrow, despite his reluctance to take on the case.[109]

McManigal offered to testify against the McNamaras and was not charged.

Darrow's work was cut out for him as he attempted to negotiate a plea agreement rather than risk trial. Darrow's argument was jeopardized when the defense team's chief investigator was arrested for bribing a juror. Darrow, too, was eventually implicated when it was revealed he was witnessed passing along funds in public. The McNamara brothers avoided trial when they pleaded guilty in December 1911. Several days later, they were sentenced to terms at San Quentin Prison. With the guilty plea from the McNamara brothers, no other union officials were ever charged. However, in 1912, the federal government brought charges against fifty-four men within the Iron Workers Union for their involvement in the union's five-year bombing campaign.[110]

The arrest and condemnation of the Iron Workers' Union in the bombing campaign resulted in loss of membership throughout the country. James B. McNamara succumbed to cancer in prison in 1941. His brother John was released from prison after nine years and rejoined the Iron Workers Union as an organizer. He would again be convicted and imprisoned for threatening a contractor if he did not hire union workers. When he was released—after having been fired from the Iron Workers Union for embezzlement—he drifted from job to job until his death in 1941.

It was a known fact that members the U.S. Secret Service as well as members of the Burns Detective Agency were operating in and around Erie in March and April, which supports the possibility of the connection between the McNamara's and the trestle bombing. This possibility was further strengthened when evidence was uncovered that tied the McNamara's to several bridge bombings that had occurred in towns in nearby Ohio.

Following the bombing, the Pennsylvania Coal Trestle was repaired and serviced hundreds of ships on the Great Lakes. Today, the coal trestle, much like most of Erie's historic waterfront, has vanished, victim of a changing environment and shipping trade. The location of where the coal trestle was is still visible on the grounds of the DonJon Shipbuilding Company.

Present-day photograph of the Anchor Line Docks. The Pennsylvania Railroad Coal Trestle would have been to the left. *Author's collection.*

If the Iron Workers Union was ultimately responsible for the bombing of the Pennsylvania Coal Trestle, it will never be fully known. 110 years have passed, and all the major players are long deceased. Despite this, the details that are known, along with the known evidence at the time from Erie City Detectives, Cleveland Police and Pennsylvania Railroad Police appear to strongly support the opinion that the Pennsylvania Coal Trestle was the victim of a campaign of domestic terrorism across the United States.

4

"AT THE MERCY OF A DESPERATE GANG"

The Five Mile Curve Train Robbery of 1911

Wintergreen Gorge winds through the Pennsylvania countryside just beyond the Erie city limits in Harborcreek Township. At nearly 3,980 feet long, it was named after the wintergreen plant, which is commonly found around the area of the gorge.[111] At its deepest point, the gorge is 250 feet deep, and on the western edge of the gorge is a line of railroad tracks that wraps around a steep embankment called Five Mile Curve.

In 1911, Five Mile Curve consisted of two pairs of railroad tracks carrying both passenger and freight trains in and out of Erie. The events that transpired on the night of June 30, 1911, were straight out of a Wild West film. Nightfall had plunged the landscape into near-total darkness as Train No. 41 of the Philadelphia & Erie Railroad chugged along at about thirty-five miles per hour, heading for Union Depot in Erie. Pulling a mail car and three passenger cars, the train carried a precious cargo: $45,000.[112]

Around 9:28 p.m., the train, helmed by engineer Albert B. Carey, passed Belle Valley and ascended a steep cliff overlooking Wintergreen Gorge and Four Mile Creek. As the train entered Five Mile Curve, fireman Leo Seachrist alerted Carey of an obstruction on the tracks seventy feet ahead. Seeing a red lantern, Carey braked the throttle as hard as he could and had almost brought the train to a standstill when the locomotive struck something, coming to a stop five or six car lengths later. Carey watched as someone climbed onto the engine. Thinking the man was a section hand, Carey called out, "What is the matter down there?"[113]

Two armed men suddenly entered the cab.

"Throw up your hands!" one of the men demanded, waving their revolvers.

Seachrist jumped from the cab almost immediately and vanished into darkness, gunshots whistling past him. Carey stepped backward out of the locomotive, hands held in the air.

Mail clerks Clarence H. Block and Martin J. Hart made their way to both ends of the car and locked the doors. Suddenly, one of the bandits made his way to the front of the car and began shooting through the window. Bullets rained down inside as head clerk Jason G. Moore ducked behind a mail case, securing a bag of registered mail, which likely saved him from being struck by one of the bullets. Hart shoved some of the registered packages under his coat and headed for the rear door.

His attention focused on the two bandits inside the cab, Carey picked up a stone, preparing to throw it at one of the bandits, but cautiously laid it on the ground as he moved forward to examine the locomotive. Both bandits then rushed Carey, and while attempting to get away, Carey fell over the edge of the embankment, injuring his back. Conductor Hugh D. Roney, who had been three cars back when he felt the train come to a sudden stop, exited the train. Getting back to his feet, Carey spotted Roney.

"Hugh!" Carey called out, "We're being held up!"

Roney rushed into the smoking car, asked for a pistol and advised the passengers the train was being held up. Roney's plea was met with scattered laughter from the passengers before another barrage of bullets tore through the air. Passengers scrambled for protection under their seats. The noise was deafening, with one passenger, Charles Freund, recalling, "It sounded as if 200 shots had been let go all at once."[114]

Mail Clerk Shot by Train Robbers

C. H. BLOCK.

Conductor Who Fought the Bandits

HUGH D. RONEY.

Top: Mail clerk Clarence H. Block. *From the* Erie Daily Times.

Bottom: Conductor Hugh D. Roney. *From the* Erie Daily Times.

Carl Anderson of Renovo, Pennsylvania, had been asleep in the smoking car until the bullets woke him up. Making his way to the front platform of the car, he stepped out to investigate, and was met by one of the bandits, whom he referred to as "a burly looking fellow wearing a mask."[115]

As Martin Hart swung the door open, preparing to exit, he found Roney engaged in a gun battle with one of the bandits. Hart jumped to the ground, picked up some rocks and hurled them at the bandits. Just as Hart was throwing one of the rocks, a gunshot pierced his right thigh. Meanwhile, one of the bandits who engaged in the gun battle with Roney attempted to flee. Roney gave pursuit toward the underbrush, firing at the bandit until he had disappeared. Carey, having also thrown rocks, disappeared into the dark as well, hoping to head for a nearby farmhouse to borrow a rifle and help. Block, who was still inside the express car guarding the mail, had been shot in the right leg.

Carl Anderson had gained control of a bandit's gun before he was tripped and rolled over the edge of the bank; his clothing becoming ensnared with some bushes, preventing him from falling to a certain death below. Within minutes, the attack had ended. Conductor Roney, who had sustained a minor injury to his leg, was able to get reach a telephone and notified Pennsylvania Railroad authorities and Erie City Police Headquarters that a robbery had taken place.

Learning that the fireman was gone, Walter C. Basset, a passenger heading home to Columbus, Ohio, made his way to the engine and started to shovel coal. As the passengers and crew waited for help, one of the female passengers, a trained nurse, assisted the wounded. At that time, Conductor Roney and the remaining train crew knew nothing about what happened to Fireman Seachrist or Engineer Carey and feared them dead.

As soon as the call came in to police headquarters, Captain William F. Detzel detailed Patrolman Willard Rice to respond to the scene. Rice, along with Deputy Sheriff James Turner, was able to gain possession of a yard engine. They set off for Five Mile Curve, apprehended Train No. 41 just east of the city and began the process of returning it to the station.

By 11:30 p.m., news of the attempted train robbery had spread like wildfire throughout the city. Men, women and children crowded the platforms at Union Depot as Train No. 41 chugged into the station. As the train came to a stop, Deputy Sheriff Frank M. Dumond and a posse of men,[116] "all of whom were armed to the teeth,"[117] boarded.

Mail clerk Block was removed from the train and loaded onto Lawrie's ambulance and transported to Hamot Hospital. Hart was taken to his

Five Mile Curve, taken in August 1915. *Author's collection.*

home at 405 West Eleventh Street. The rest of the crew who stayed behind later learned that Albert Carey had managed to track down help and was resting at his home. Conductor Roney, suffering from his badly bruised leg, refused to go home until all the necessary reports were completed.[118] When passenger Carl Anderson reached the New Morton House, his clothing was torn to shreds and his trousers ruined. Speaking briefly with reporters, he stated that he would continue his journey to Chicago, undeterred.

Once the search of Train No. 41 was completed, Dumond's posse was transported halfway to the scene of the robbery aboard a passenger train. Upon disembarking, they transferred to a yard engine and secluded themselves in a caboose until they reached the intersection with Shannon Road, almost exactly where the obstruction had occurred.

By midnight, Five Mile Curve was alive with intensity. Dumond and his men left the caboose and were met by Lieutenant William Beiter and Detective Everett of the Philadelphia & Erie Railroad. Lieutenant of Police Robert Cruthers and detectives from the nearby Lake Shore & Michigan Southern Railroad were also on the scene and had begun patrolling the woods and fields nearby. Dumond and Beiter sent the remaining men to begin a customary search of nearby houses, woods and fields within the vicinity of the tracks for additional clues.

Beiter and his men had a jump start on the investigation—they were actually nearby investigating another portion of the tracks, waiting for another freight train to pass, and they had been alerted the day prior that some individual—or individuals—had intentionally removed spikes from a section of the rails.

In a nearby shed used by workmen from the St. John Kanty College, detectives found a lock ripped from a toolbox and tools missing from inside. The lock of a nearby shanty was also found to be missing. Meanwhile, in Erie, around 3:00 a.m., Clarence A. Davis was awakened at his residence at 619 East Twelfth Street. Looking out to the rear of his yard, he noticed three men walking up the alley. One of the men appeared to be clutching his arm as if injured.

As the sun rose over the fields and woods of Wintergreen Gorge and Five Mile Curve, Dumond and his men called off their search and headed back to Erie, sore and tired. Beiter and his men remained near Shannon Road, where they remained throughout the day. Every individual who passed was questioned thoroughly, and later that day detectives from the U.S. Postal Department joined the search for the attempted thieves along with the Pennsylvania State Police. Additionally, the Erie Police Department detailed Detective Sergeants Richard Crotty and Officers Reagan, Casey and Wittenberg to the case.

It was a miracle that in the massive barrage of lead that had struck Train No. 41, nobody was killed. The most seriously injured, Clarence Block, was tended to quickly, and he would make a full recovery. Martin Hart's wound in the right thigh didn't prevent him from walking home from the Union Depot. Arriving at home, Hart called a doctor to his residence, and a lead pellet was removed and the wound dressed. With the help of a cane, Hart left aboard a special train that morning to offer his assistance.

As detectives scoured the countryside for clues, it was clear the bandits had not escaped unscathed. Near the scene of the robbery, detectives found a piece of glass with a bloody fingerprint on it. The fingerprint, that of a thumb and palm lines in blood, was later determined to have come from when one of the bandits fired into the window of the express car; in the process, he had lacerated part of his hand.

This was confirmed by mail clerk Moore, who stated that after gunshots started to ring out, he began to take steps to protect the mail. Moore said to a reporter, "It was up to me to save that mail and I intended to do it no matter what happened. Just as I gathered up the mail, one of the fellows put his fists through the glass and pulled away the curtain that I had jerked down when the firing commenced. I could see that his hand was bloody as he thrust it through the broken glass."[119]

Union Depot, Erie, Pennsylvania. *Author's collection.*

Despite a review of the damage to the railroad cars and locomotive, investigators could never pinpoint how many shots were exchanged between the bandits and the train crew. A member of the crew, when questioned by detectives, testified that about forty to fifty shots had been fired, whereas additional crew and passengers believed it was more like two hundred shots. Determining how many bandits involved was also puzzling detectives. Members of the crew were confident that there were at least four, at most six men involved. The *Times* released a description of four of the men in the morning edition of July 1, 1911:

> *No. 1—Five feet six inches tall, wore a brown stiff hat, had black mustache and weighed about 130 pounds.*
> *No. 2—About six feet tall, smooth face, light complexion.*
> *No. 3—About five feet eight inches tall, weight 140 pounds. Wore a cap.*
> *No. 4—About six feet tall, weighed 150 pounds, smooth face and wore a brown soft hat.*[120]

Detectives also located two sticks of dynamite in a basket lying under a tree down in Four Mile Creek, roughly two hundred yards from the holdup. The dynamite was covered with a Polish newspaper issued on March 17, 1911. This basket and its contents matched statements from farmers who lived about a half a mile away and saw two men, resembling foreigners, carrying a basket of similar design and contents. Daybreak also provided a clear look at how the obstruction had been set up. The *Times* explained in detail:

> It was the red lights, it is asserted, that brought Engineer Abe Carey almost to a standstill with his train, and not the presence of the obstruction placed on the track. The pile of ties, surmounted by two telegraph poles, laid crosswise the obstruction, was out of the range of vision of the engineer from his side of the cab in rounding the curve which is most acute at that point.[121]

Police had already begun to form an idea who the bandits were but refused to release information other than to say that the work was done by a "desperate gang," considered "raw," attempting to blast their way through the express car, only to become panic-stricken when the crew and passengers began to fight back, spoiling their plans. Later in the day, Clarence Davis spoke with a neighbor, Simon Reed, who lived at 631 East Twelfth Street and told him of the strange occurrence during the early hours that morning. Both men then entered the alley, where they spotted blood on the street, near Reed Street.

The Erie Police Department had also taken steps to pursue those involved, ordering a roundup of floaters and strangers who were unable to provide a satisfactory account of their whereabouts the night previous. These orders stretched to all points on the Philadelphia & Erie Division as well as to that of the Lake Shore, Bessemer and Nickel Plate Railroads, all of which pledged to assist the investigation. Walter Mooney and James Carroll, two men arrested by Detective Sergeant Richard Crotty that morning in a raid on a hobo camp near the Chemical Works, were found to have not been involved and were told that they would be released once their five-day term of imprisonment expired.

When police determined that one of the bandits had sustained injuries that would require attention, they sent a notice to all physicians within the county to notify them of any individuals who had been recently treated with injuries from a revolver or glass. Dr. John Ackerman, 9 West Eleventh Street, contacted the police and said that on the night of the holdup at about 10:30 p.m. he believed he treated one of the bandits at his office. The man had a lacerated thumb that appeared to have been cut by glass. He spoke English but with a foreign accent and claimed he was from New

Scene of the Five Mile Curve holdup, photographed by Walter Kiedaisch. *From the* Erie Daily Times.

York. The wound was supposedly from getting involved in two gangs fighting near Orchard Beach, North East.

When pressed for a description, Ackerman recalled him being about twenty-five years old and seemingly in a hurry.[122] Additional searches of Wintergreen Gorge and Four Mile Creek yielded only a brown slouch hat, missing the label, with only an identifying mark, a size 7¼. Police made additional arrests and looked into suspicious individuals; however, these leads withered as the investigation dragged on. The postmaster general, Frank Harris Hitchcock, issued a special order offering a reward of $1,000 for information leading to the arrest.[123] The solution to the mystery, up to that point, was anybody's guess.

The city and countryside were on edge. This was clear when detectives from the Pennsylvania Railroad were alerted around nine o'clock on the night of July 7, 1911, that a local gang of tough-looking individuals resembling the bandits were congregating around Five Mile Curve. The authorities, with assistance from Erie City detectives, were immediately called to action. The men gained possession of a switch engine and notified the train dispatcher to tell Train No. 41, at that time in Belle Valley, to halt until men arrived.[124] When detectives arrived, they found no gangs, just a countryside full of detectives.

As the investigation continued, additional leads and angles dried up. The investigation sustained a major loss when George W. Vernes, inspector of police with the Pennsylvania Railroad, succumbed to pneumonia on July 29, 1911. The investigation briefly ceased until a section man who was cutting the grass near the railroad bed where the holdup took place located a .32-caliber Colt revolver. A belt, minus the buckle, was also found,[125] along with a homemade bomb, fastened together with a gas pipe. The news breathed new life into the investigation, and by August 1, 1911, police had begun to zero in on three suspects and an arrest was imminent.

A Desperate Gang

Frank J. Winicki was arrested in Buffalo, New York, on August 1, 1911, while working at the C.&B. Docks. The arrest, accomplished by Lieutenant Robert Cruthers of the Lake Shore Railroad, was due in part to the ongoing investigation in Erie. Authorities learned from Winicki's family and associates that he mentioned "shooting a fellow as he rolled down the bank."[126]

An investigation into Winicki's whereabouts revealed that he left the city of Erie the night after the attempted holdup. When arrested, Winicki demanded a hearing and fiercely denied being involved in the attempted holdup. Brought before Commissioner Keating in Buffalo to answer to the charges, Winicki came prepared and summoned several co-workers, who testified he had been working there on June 30.

The government also brought witnesses. Carl Anderson, who grappled with one of the bandits before being almost thrown over the edge to his death, appeared as a witness. Anderson was positive Winicki was the individual he fought that night. Conductor Hugh Roney and fireman Leo Seachrist also appeared. While Commissioner Keating did not have the authority to hold Winicki for the federal grand jury or transfer him to another federal judicial district, he advised he would relay necessary recommendations to the district judge in Buffalo who had the proper jurisdiction.[127]

Winicki would be held and transferred to the Allegheny County Courthouse in Pittsburgh to stand trial for his role in the attempted holdup.

Frank Winicki. *National Archives.*

As for police in the City of Erie, Frank Winicki was someone they were all too familiar with.

Franciszek Winicki was born to Andrzej and Elizabeth Mazanna on January 14, 1884, in Milwaukee, Wisconsin. The family had moved to Erie by 1900 and resided in the Polish neighborhood of St. Stanislaus Parish at 455 East Fifteenth Street. Winicki married Mary Wasielewska on September 19, 1904, at St. Stanislaus Roman Catholic Church in Erie. To support his family, Winicki worked shop jobs, primarily as a moulder at an iron foundry. Winicki's first major run-in with the law occurred when he threw Officer John Fletcher down a stairwell when Fletcher attempted to arrest him,[128] severely injuring the officer's spine.[129]

Winicki again found himself in trouble with the law when arrested in 1906 and charged with assault and battery against his wife and for surety of the peace,[130] although the charges were dropped when Winicki appeared before Erie mayor Robert J. Saltsman, promising to improve his behavior.

Winicki was still working as a moulder in the iron foundry in the beginning of 1911. At the time, Winicki's wife was pregnant with their fifth child. Also around this time, Winicki started to become acquainted with two infamous known criminals: John "Bull" Trinowski and Leo "Lefty" Kendziora. Police confirmed that Trinowski and Kendziora were in Winicki's company the day of the holdup.[131]

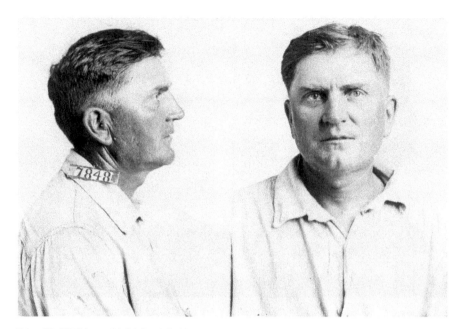

John "Bull" Trinowski. *National Archives.*

John "Bull" Trinowski was born around 1876 in Pennsylvania to parents who had emigrated from West Prussia. Not much is known about him until February 2, 1897, when Trinowski and an accomplice, John Falkowski, held up Leo Montgomery near a bridge that spanned Mill Creek at East Eleventh and Holland Streets. As Falkowski searched Montgomery, Bull shot his victim through the eye. Both men fled the scene. Trinowski was arrested two days later, and Falkowski was on the run for about a year until he was apprehended in a saloon on the east side of the city.

Trinowski was put on trial before Judge Emory Walling, who found him guilty of Montgomery's murder and sentenced Trinowski to the Western Penitentiary. He had only been out of prison for a short time when the holdup occurred on File Mile Curve. When the police fixed Trinowski as being the ringleader of the holdup, friends claimed he was innocent, telling the police he had done what he could to live an honest lifestyle since his release and was not in Erie around the time of the holdup.

Leo "Lefty" Kendziora was a well-known criminal to Erie Police as well. He was born on December 8, 1887, to Jozef and Mary (née Went) Kendziora in Graudenz, West Prussia.[132] Upon immigrating to the United States, Kendziora's family settled in Erie. Kendziora was a petty thief and criminal and had accumulated quite a lengthy rap sheet since his teenage years.

With Winicki safely locked away in Pittsburgh, police set out about the dangerous task of pursuing Kendziora and Trinowski for their roles in the attempted holdup, a hunt that would soon escalate in further mayhem.

A man by the name of Bert James was walking on East Thirteenth Street, between Ash and Reed Streets, on the night of August 22, 1911, when he was stopped by two men aiming revolvers. The thieves rifled James's pockets, taking twenty-eight cents before one of the men turned, spotting someone approaching. It was none other than Lieutenant William Beiter. Recognizing the officer, one of the armed men fired a shot, nearly missing his head.[133]

By then a crowd had gathered near the corner, and the thieves fled. Beiter refrained from firing back, as he feared striking an innocent bystander, and both men escaped. Beiter and James went downtown to police headquarters and provided descriptions of the men. Beiter instantly recognized both men as none other than Bull Trinowski and Lefty Kendziora, with Trinowski being the one who fired the shot at him.

It was revealed by the *Times* the following day that both men were part of the gang that held up the Philadelphia & Erie train on July 30, 1911, and police were of the opinion that they were still operating in and about the city. This was supported by the fact Kendziora and Trinowski were identified as two of five men responsible for the robbery of four men at the Cascade Street railroad crossing on the morning of August 24.[134] Following the holdup, Patrolman Louis Scalise was made aware of the robbery and pursued the five bandits as they ran west on the Lake Shore railroad tracks. Scalise and the bandits exchanged shots before they escaped.

Following the actions of Kendziora, Trinowski and their gang, the police beefed up patrols. But with the increased presence on the streets, things suddenly ceased. Some thought the gang was lying low or had migrated to another city. There was also a growing belief that maybe the rest of those responsible for the crimes would never again be apprehended.

Toward the end of September, Chief of Police Edward Wagner learned that Leo "Lefty" Kendziora had been arrested in Painesville, Ohio, charged with highway robbery, assault and intent to commit murder; he had used the alias "Frank Davis." Both Kendziora and an accomplice later broke out of jail but were recaptured in Ashtabula, Ohio. When Wagner was told of Kendziora's recapture, he sent Patrolman Anthony Mozdyniewicz along with Philadelphia & Erie Railroad lieutenant William Beiter to Ashtabula to see if Davis was Kendziora.

On September 23, 1911, when Mozdyniewicz and Beiter arrived at the Ashtabula County Jail, they were greeted by Lefty Kendziora, who laughed

Erie, Pennsylvania, as it would have appeared in 1911. *Library of Congress.*

upon seeing both policemen. Although wanted in Erie by investigators for the U.S. Postal Service, who had taken over the Five Mile investigation, Kendziora was returned to Painesville to stand trial. Ohio authorities informed Chief Wagner they would keep an eye on Kendziora in the future.

Kendziora was convicted in October that year for his crimes and sentenced to two years in the Ohio State Penitentiary in Columbus.[135] It was rumored that at the end of Kendziora's term in the penitentiary, he would be arrested by authorities and charged for his role in the train holdup.

It was on the afternoon of December 17, 1911, that Officer Frank Cichocki was provided with a tip that John "Bull" Trinowski was seen near Dunn's old Brick Yard on East Twelfth Street. Cichocki phoned headquarters and notified Chief William Detzel about the tip.

Chief Detzel's orders on apprehending Trinowski were clear: "Do not take any chances with this fellow. If he shows fight, shoot at him. Take him alive if you can, but don't take any chances. Get him before he gets you."[136] Detectives Richard Crotty and Lambertine Pinney were tasked with getting Trinowski and supported by Officers Martin and McCallion, who would rendezvous with Cichocki.

The officers made their way to the old brickyard and surrounded the premises, drawing their revolvers when they spotted Trinowski in the company of two men. Police apprehended Trinowski without incident and transported him to police headquarters. At first, Trinowski denied that he was the individual the police were looking for, but at the station he was positively identified by Patrolman Anthony Mozdyniewicz before being turned over to Pennsylvania Railroad inspector Charles W. Bathurst and Deputy U.S. Marshal Robert J. Firman.

The following day, Trinowski went before U.S. Commissioner Frank Grant and was arraigned and charged with his involvement in the attempted train robbery.[137] Trinowski's capture was welcomed by U.S. District Attorney John M. Jordan, who had been preparing for the upcoming trial against Winicki.

On December 26, 1911, Commissioner Grant was notified that the government would try both Winicki and Trinowski in Erie at a session of the U.S. District Court the second week in January 1912. Trinowski, held at the Erie County Jail, would remain in custody until his trial. Winicki, however, was out on bail awaiting the trial. Trinowski was eager for the trial and had attempted to learn what the government had against him in terms of evidence. A confidant of Trinowski's told a reporter, "They'll have to 'job him' if they'll connect 'Bull' up with that affair."[138]

By the end of 1911, the jury in the trial against Trinowski and Winicki was drawn and ready. Winicki also appeared confident that the trial would end in an acquittal for both men. District Attorney Jordan had kept mum about the details the government would present in the trial, and how it would all play out was anyone's guess.

The *Times* issued a more pessimistic opinion: "From what it is stated the railroad detectives have in the line of evidence against either of the defendants their conviction is improbable."[139]

"I Am as Innocent as a Newborn Child"

The trial against John "Bull" Trinowski and Frank Winicki started at 2:00 p.m. on January 8, 1912, before Judge Charles P. Orr at the Old Federal Building in Downtown Erie. Attorney Robert H. Chinnock represented Winicki, while attorney P. Dale Hyner represented Trinowski. With the government calling over forty witnesses,[140] the defense's plan focused on presenting alibis to discredit testimonies that placed Winicki and Trinowski at the scene of the robbery—a difficult task considering the overwhelming evidence against both men.

U.S. District Attorney John M. Jordan, who tried the case against Gilbert Perkins and Charles Franklin in the Black Hand Fraud Trial in 1911, opened for the government by building a step-by-step narrative about what occurred the night of the attempted robbery. Jordan opened with the witness statements the following day, January 9, with Leroy J. Fairbanks. The supervisor with the Philadelphia & Erie Railroad testified about what he witnessed while in

The U.S. Federal Courthouse located at the corner of South Park Row and State Street. *Erie County Historical Society.*

one of the passenger cars. Next was C.L.P. Russell, an assistant supervisor of the Pennsylvania Railroad, who testified how he and Fairbanks made a diagram of the curve and scene of the holdup. The map was then produced to the courtroom and its details explained to the jury.

Michael Falvey, a track foreman for the Pennsylvania Railroad, recalled that the day after the holdup he had found spikes pulled out of the rails on the north side of the tracks. The splice belts, Falvey continued, had also been loosened, which would, in theory, cause the rail to buckle and dislodge the train from the track. Falvey also testified that on the morning before the holdup he had located sixteen spikes that had been removed from the south side of the track, along with an additional fourteen spikes. It was clear, he continued, that someone had deliberately removed them. That morning, the lock of the nearby tool house had been broken into. On the morning of July 1, after the holdup had taken place, Falvey stated that someone had broken into the same tool house and had taken some tools, including a claw bar and several wrenches. The wrenches were later located near where the obstruction had been laid on the tracks, Falvey told attorney Jordan.

The theatrics of the trial reached their height when Captain Rose of the Pennsylvania Railroad carefully produced one of the sticks of dynamite that had been found near the location of the holdup and handed it to District Attorney Jordan. It was still wrapped in the pages of a Polish newspaper. Before District Attorney Jordan could proceed, Judge Orr ordered the explosives removed from the courthouse, telling Jordan they would not be needed for the trial.

Falvey continued his testimony, telling Jordan that an inspection of the gorge had been performed on July 1, and it was clear that a struggle had taken place at the spot. Captain H.W. Rose took the stand next and confirmed that he had been at the scene of the holdup the following morning with Inspector Vernes and the police. Captain Rose elaborated on the bomb, saying that it contained two sticks of 40 percent dynamite with a fuse and cap attached, prepared to detonate.

Fireman Leo Seachrist was called to the stand following Captain Rose and positively identified Trinowski and Winicki as two of the bandits. Seachrist was put through a grueling cross-examination by attorney Chinnock, who attempted to discredit Seachrist's identification of Winicki. Seachrist refused to budge, stating that the bandit who held a revolver in his face possessed a peculiar voice, especially when he pronounced the letter *S*. That voice, Seachrist declared, was the same when he identified Winicki in Buffalo.[141]

Jordan called the remainder of the train crew that morning, and they "testified to the exciting circumstances on the night of June 30."[142] Albert Carey and Hugh Roney offered their testimonies before the 12:30 p.m. recess.

The afternoon was devoted to testimony from John Alamenczak. Alamenczak testified that on June 29, the night preceding the holdup, he was heading home at a late hour when he spotted four men coming through a field near East Thirteenth and Wayne Streets by the Stearn Manufacturing

Company. The men, Alamenczak continued, were talking about having "hard luck that it didn't go over after they pulled so many spikes out."[143]

Two of the men, Alamenczak said, were Winicki and Trinowski. As they came into view, Trinowski handed a claw-bar to Winicki, who then hid it under a chicken coop. It was Trinowski who spotted Alamenczak and said, "There comes a live one, we might get some coin from him,"[144] and before Alamenczak could react, Trinowski pressed a revolver against Alamenczak's face. Winicki knew Alamenczak and insisted to Trinowski that he was all right, but his request was ignored. Alamenczak, accompanied by a child, pleaded for mercy. Trinowski demanded fifty cents before searching through Alamenczak's pockets, taking fifteen cents, a pipe and a paper of tobacco.

The evidence was damaging, and an attempt by attorney Chinnock to put Alamenczak through a rigorous cross-examination refused to shake his story. Alamenczak further cemented his testimony against Trinowski and Winicki when he confirmed that prior to him being held up, he heard one of the men mention something about dynamite, to which Winicki remarked that his father had some that he used to blow up stumps. When Chinnock asked Alamenczak why he never reported any of this to the police, Alamenczak said he feared for his life.

On January 10, 1912, attorney Jordan called more witnesses who continued to chip away at Winicki and Trinowski and their supposed alibis. He began with Clarence A. Davis, awakened in the early hours of July 1 by three men walking behind his home. Next was Simon Reed, who testified about finding blood spots with Davis near the alley where the three men were seen.

Post office inspector L.A. Johnson, who handled the investigation for the government, was called next. Johnson testified that he visited a nearby physician, Dr. Melchior Mszanowski, and inquired if anyone had been treated that night. Witness J.A. Wheeler, a traveling salesman, testified that on the afternoon of June 30, while driving to Belle Valley, he witnessed Frank Winicki and Leo "Lefty" Kendziora near the Pennsylvania Railroad tracks. C.F. Kennell with the Pennsylvania Railroad Detective Department testified that on June 26, while on duty in Erie near the Lake Shore railroad tracks, he saw three men standing on the Lake Shore right of way. While traveling out of Erie to Warren on a freight train later that night, Kennell saw five men near Five Mile Curve. Three of the men attempted to get on the train but were unsuccessful. Kennell identified the three men as Kendziora, Trinowski and Winicki.

Philip J. McCallion, of 344 East Fifteenth Street, was next called and testified that on the afternoon of June 30 he spotted Kendziora, Trinowski,

Winick and another man he did not know on East Twenty-Sixth Street near the Pennsylvania Railroad tracks. John Skowronski, in the vicinity of the Erie City Iron Works, testified that on June 25 he saw Winicki, Trinowski and four other men nearby. It was at 11:00 a.m. that attorney Jordan advised that the government rested its case, setting the stage for the defense attorneys to present their case.

Attorney Chinnock started the defense's position by asking the court to instruct the jury to return a verdict of not guilty due to the government having not sufficiently proven its case against both men. Chinnock supported this request based on provisions of the penal code under which the indictment in Pittsburgh had been drawn. Judge Orr overruled the motion.

Continuing, Chinnock informed the jury that there would be evidence shown that it was a fact that both Winicki and Trinowski were not in Erie at the time of the holdup. The first witness called was Frank Winicki, who took the stand on his own behalf. Winicki claimed that he had left Erie on June 29 and went to Buffalo to visit his brother-in-law. On July 6, Winicki claimed, he obtained employment under the name Frank Williams in Buffalo and only learned about the holdup on July 10 when reading the *Buffalo Courier*. During his cross-examination by attorney Jordan, Winicki claimed that all of the witnesses who had identified him were simply lying and that he had never been around the vicinity of Five Mile Curve. The defense next called Konstanty Waycicki, a witness who claimed he had met Frank Winicki in Buffalo on June 29, 1911, in a saloon on Michigan Street.

Following the recess for lunch, John "Bull" Trinowski took the stand in his own defense, claiming that he was nowhere near Erie when the holdup occurred and was in Sistersville, West Virginia. Despite his testimony, however, Trinowski was not able to provide any evidence to support his claim. Trinowski admitted that he had been previously incarcerated before in the Western Penitentiary for murder and wrapped up his testimony around 2:30 p.m. Following Trinowski's testimony, the defense rested.

In his rebuttal to the defense, attorney Jordan recalled several more witnesses and broke down, piece by piece, the testimonies of Winicki and Trinowski. Jordan brought up Winicki's testimony that he left Erie two days before the holdup and was not in Erie until after he had been released from jail in Pittsburgh. Jordan countered Winicki's own words by recalling those of the Polish neighbor who testified that they saw Winicki on June 29. Lieutenant Beiter was re-called and testified about his shoot-out with Trinowski and Kendziora on August 23 on the Lake Shore tracks. Finally, Jordan wrapped up the rebuttal with testimony from several officers from the

Erie Police Department who attested to Trinowski's reputation. With court adjourning for the day, both sides prepared for closing arguments.

As court opened on the morning of January 11, 1912, Trinowski's attorney, Dale Hyner, presented a list of law points to the court, only to have them all overruled, save for the point instructing the jury about the meaning of reasonable doubt. Hyner was followed by Chinnock, who summed up the defense. When discussing the testimony that identified Winicki and Trinowski as two of the bandits, Chinnock discredited the accounts as being nothing more than "a testimony of identification" and told members of the jury that Carl Anderson and John Alamenczak could not be believed. Chinnock informed the jury that they had no choice to find both men not guilty due to their alibis having proven that they were in West Virginia and New York.

At 11:00 a.m., District Attorney Jordan opened his closing remarks with a passionate plea for conviction against Trinowski and Winicki. If Train No. 41 had happened to roll over the steep embankment at Five Mile Curve after striking the obstruction, Jordan proclaimed, dozens of innocent men and women would likely have been killed. He also highlighted the testimony of John Alamenczak. The most important evidence, Jordan told the jury, was testimony of numerous witnesses who were able to place Trinowski and Winicki at the scene of the crime and asked to find a verdict of guilty.

Judge Orr began his charge to the jury at 12:06 p.m., speaking of the five counts in the indictment, taking the time to explain each count separately. Orr instructed the jury to carefully consider the evidence and exercise their best judgment as they normally would in their daily routines. Judge Orr concluded his remarks and at 12:27 p.m., and the jury started their deliberations.

At 2:29 p.m., the jury informed the court they had reached a verdict in just under three hours.

Marshal E. Hadsell Porter escorted Winicki and Trinowski from the Erie County Jail, and by the time both defendants entered the courtroom the jury had already been seated. Judge Orr read the verdict: guilty in manner and form as indicted on all counts. Winicki turned pale while Trinowski looked on stoically. Once Judge Orr finished, U.S. attorney Jordan moved for sentencing, and both men were brought before the judge, who said, "John Trinowski and Frank Winicki, it is now my duty to pass sentence upon you. You have been found guilty in manner and form as indicated and I believe you have had a fair trial. John Trinowski, is there any reason why the sentence of this court should not be passed upon you?"

"I am as innocent as a newborn child," Trinowski responded. "I hope in time to be able to establish my innocence."

Orr turned to Winicki, repeating his question.

"I throw myself on the mercy of the court,"[145] Winicki responded.

Judge Orr replied,

> *There is nothing for the court to do in this case but pass the sentence that is fixed for the punishment of the offense you have been convicted of, by an act of congress. It is a severe penalty and were I to fix the time of your imprisonment, I do not believe I would pass as severe a sentence. I sentence each of you to the Federal prison at Leavenworth, Kansas, for a period of twenty-five years.*

Upon hearing the sentence, Winicki's wife sobbed. Attempting to rise from the chair, she screamed, only to fall backward. As both men were led from the room, Winicki leaned over, kissing his wife goodbye.

The following morning, Marshal Porter, accompanied by three deputies, waited with the prisoners at Union Depot. Upon arriving in Pittsburgh, both Winicki and Trinowski were to be taken to the Allegheny County Jail and remain there until arrangements for the final transfer to Fort Leavenworth were completed. A reporter from the *Erie Daily Times* described the scene at Union Depot as Winicki bid farewell to his wife and children:

> *It was a sad scene when husband and wife bade each other goodbye—the husband and father was leaving for far away Kansas, where he was to spend a quarter century in separate and solitary confinement. Tears were streaming down Winicki's face when he boarded the train and the wife and three children were huddled together in the corner of the waiting room—crying. Stooping over, Winiecki kissed his wife and children good-bye and then the party boarded the train.*[146]

As for Trinowski, he remained silent, with the same look he had possessed throughout his trial. He entered the railroad carriage that morning without making a statement. John Trinowski and Frank Winicki would arrive at Fort Leavenworth Prison on January 22, 1912, labeled as prisoners no. 7848 and no. 7849, respectively.

Frank Winicki was paroled on July 18, 1920. After his release, he returned to Erie, but by that time his marriage had broken down and he soon found himself divorced. Winicki later moved to Chicago, Illinois, where he found employment as a baker. He married again in 1927 and died on August 26, 1954, at the age of seventy.

While at the Ohio State Penitentiary in 1912, Leo "Lefty" Kendziora and four prisoners attempted to escape. Kendziora was shot in the scalp in his bid for freedom. In 1913, he was back in Erie and once again found himself arrested and charged with receiving stolen goods. Kendziora would never be brought to trial for his role in the attempted holdup and remained in Erie well into the 1920s. From there he seems to have vanished from records entirely and is last known to have been alive in 1952.

A photograph of Frank Winicki, following his release from Fort Leavenworth Prison. *National Archives.*

John Trinowski was paroled on December 20, 1924, at the age of forty-eight. Once he was released, he disappeared from records and his whereabouts remain unknown.

When Hugh D. Roney retired in 1932 after fifty years of service with the Pennsylvania Railroad, he was regarded as one of the most well-known men in the city of Erie, not only by locals but also travelers who met him during his tenure as conductor. Roney remembered the holdup of Train No. 41 as the most thrilling experience of his career.[147] He died on March 14, 1940, at the age of seventy-eight and is buried in Laurel Hill Cemetery in Millcreek Township, Pennsylvania.

Albert Carey was commended by the Philadelphia & Erie Railroad for his heroism the night No. 41 was held up. The last of five brothers, all railroad men, Carey chalked up an impressive career of almost forty-eight years as an engineer with over thirty-five years of experience hauling passenger trains before his retirement. He was considered one of the last of the "Grand Old Men of the Philadelphia & Erie Railroad," and at the time of his death in December 1921, hundreds flocked to Erie for his funeral.

Five Mile Curve still exists today, although only one set of railroad tracks runs along the edge overlooking Four Mile Creek. The once vibrant fields and farmlands have been replaced with residential housing and woodlots. Railroad traffic has declined on the curve since 1911. The gorge below, and Four Mile Creek, however, remain a popular attraction for families and college students from the nearby Penn State Behrend campus during the summer months.

If only the trees and rails could talk, one can imagine the story they would tell of Train No. 41 coming around the bend on Five Mile Curve and its inevitable date with history on June 30, 1911.

5

"I DON'T DARE SQUEAL"

The Blackwood Potato Patch Murder and the Unsolved Murder of Anthony Sperandeo

B y the summer of 1920, the effects of Prohibition had spread throughout the country, especially within cities along the Great Lakes. The federal government had been caught off guard when cities refused to enforce the new law and found themselves struggling to combat a rise in crime. The city of Erie was not immune to the effects of Prohibition. Positioned between Cleveland, Buffalo and Pittsburgh, Erie would become an important player in criminal activity throughout the Roaring Twenties.

The morning of August 14, 1920, would become another gruesome footnote in Erie's Prohibition criminal history.

Around 7:30 a.m., farmers Leo Randall and Frank Scheal were traveling into Erie to market.[148] The air, humid due to heavy rainfall the night before, clung to the men's clothing as they walked along Zimmerman Road, passing along the Pennsylvania & Erie Railroad woods and the fields and orchards belonging to local farmer James Blackwood. It was while walking along the dirt road that distinct blood marks in the roadway drew their attention.

Following the blood, which led about twenty to thirty feet into a nearby potato patch, the men made a shocking discovery: the remains of what appeared to be a person lying on their left side, with most of their clothing and features charred beyond recognition.

Alarmed, the farmers fled the field and called police.

Detective William H. Sandusky and Patrolman Edward Steiner were the first on scene when they arrived around 8:00 a.m. Inspecting the bloodstains, both men determined that a struggle had taken place before the body was

The charred remains found in John Blackwood's potato patch. *From the* Erie Daily Times.

dragged into the field. Police also noted the tracks of an automobile in the road, traveling east, which had skidded to a complete halt right next to the spots of blood in the road.

Detectives George Barber, Frank Gaczkowski and Paul Luthringer arrived, joining Sandusky and Steiner at the scene. Venturing into the field, the men came face to face with the body. Six feet away was a discarded two-quart water bottle[149] that had been used to carry gasoline. Two hours later, a large boilermaker's hammer, encrusted with blood, was found embedded in the south bank of the road nearby.[150]

The body, although heavily burned, was identified as male. A quick inspection revealed the victim's trousers, socks and shoes were left untouched by the flames. The clothing was reported as being of "cheap" quality. Next to the body, a broken piece of sumac tree was found, stained with blood and slightly burned.

Continuing with the theory that a struggle had preceded the man's murder, police started to form the opinion that once the body had been dragged into the field, it was set ablaze to hide the victim's identity. The two-quart water bottle was scorched, leading police to believe that the killer—or killers—had been burned in their endeavor to torch the body. Police believed the broken sumac limb was used to stir the fire and that the boilermaker's hammer was involved. The victim's shabby clothing indicated it was unlikely the murder was robbery-related, although this belief was not shared by every detective present.

Soon, onlookers appeared on the road, gawking at the grisly scene. A photographer from the *Erie Daily Times* photographed the remains, which would be flashed on the front pages two days later. When notified about the murder, Chief Detzel assigned Detective Sergeants George Christoph, Ganzer and Barber to the case to assist William Sandusky along with Patrolmen Ralph Waidley and Steiner. Detectives and state troopers from the Pennsylvania State Police helped assist at the scene.

James Blackwood, the farmer on whose property the crime occurred, lived about two hundred yards away. He told police that the previous night he retired to bed at eight o'clock and had not heard anything. He became aware of the murder when notified by the police and neighbors. Officers fanned out to the nearby farms to see if any farmhands were missing but learned there were no credible cases of any missing persons. They also looked into crimes that happened on the Blackwood farm in the past. This, too, yielded no connection.[151]

A clue to the possible time of the murder arose: nearby neighbors reported that between 10:30 and 11:00 p.m., they had spotted a fire on Blackwood's property. The witnesses claimed that they chalked it up to being a bonfire and thought nothing about it. Witnesses also claimed that they saw two

Curious onlookers flock to John Blackwood's potato patch the day after the murder. *From the Erie Daily Times.*

automobiles on Zimmerman Road that night, one being an Auburn model vehicle. Erie County coroner Theobald M. Flynn arrived on the scene, immediately pronounced the victim as deceased and had him removed to Brugger's Undertaking and Funeral Parlors on East Ninth Street. As the *Erie Daily Times* and *Erie Dispatch* raced to go to press, the police were already overwhelmed with questions and information.

Two witnesses came forward upon hearing the news of the body being discovered. Arthur Brandler, 749 Rosedale Avenue, and Ethel Sandstrom, 2910 Holland Street, had driven past the field several times while waiting for Ethel's brother, Axel, who was calling at the William Hess farm, which adjoined the Blackwood property. Both Brandler and Sandstrom told police that they spotted the fire—like the others, they believed it was a bonfire—and two automobiles parked on the side of the road, one identified as a Ford.

According to Sandstrom, one of the vehicles was stationary, facing toward Erie. Two individuals were seen in the front seat, although Sandstrom unable to distinguish any features or if they were men or women. The other car was parked in a driveway east of the field, roughly a city block from the burning body. Brandler told police when passing he smelled the distinct odor of burning clothes despite the pouring rain.

Sandstrom and Brandler left the Hess farm around midnight after retrieving Sandstrom's brother and, upon passing the field, noted that the fire had died down. As they were heading into Erie, the vehicle that had been seen parked east of Blackwood's potato patch suddenly roared past Brandler's vehicle, racing toward Erie. It was when Brandler's vehicle reached East Twenty-Eighth Street that the witnesses spotted a man, his face hidden with a newspaper, walking rapidly east toward the Blackwood farm.

As police sought to understand the crime, coroner Flynn began the arduous task of an autopsy and identifying the murder victim at Brugger's Undertaking Parlor. The man, Flynn later remarked, had been soaked with gasoline before being set on fire. Death was due to the victim having been struck, most likely by the boilermaker's hammer, in the occipital region, which lacerated the scalp and fractured his skull. Death, Flynn noted, would have been instantaneous, and he believed that when the body was set ablaze the victim was already deceased.

The victim was roughly five feet, four inches tall, possibly of Italian heritage or ancestry, and had brown hair. His features, blackened and slightly charred by flames, would prove to make identification difficult. It was noted that he had small ears and his teeth were in excellent condition with fillings in the back molars.

Brugger's Undertaking Parlors as they would have appeared in 1920. *Courtesy of Brugger Funeral Homes.*

The clothing failed to reveal any clues to the identity of the dead man. The gray-black striped trousers, almost entirely intact, were burned around the waist and pockets. A search of the pockets revealed no items that would help assist with the identity. The victim's shoes were tan-colored Selz shoes, an army-style footwear with rubber heels. Remnants of a cheap black belt were found around the waist. The shirt was practically in tatters, and the dead man possessed no coat.

That afternoon calls had started to come in at Brugger's Undertaking Parlor, one of which included an individual who thought the dead victim might be his missing son. He later found out he was mistaken after the body was measured. Later that night, Coroner Flynn presided over the inquest. Detective Sandusky and Patrolman Steiner were called as witnesses, as were the farmers who located the body. The prime witnesses were Arthur Brandler and Ethel Sandstrom, who provided their testimony about the events of the night prior to the jury.

The jury returned a verdict that the police had anticipated: "By murderous intent by a person or persons at present unknown."[152]

Flynn reported that the body would be held for several days to allow for possible identification. Rumors and speculation spread throughout Erie and the countryside. Had the infamous Mafia entrenched itself in Erie? Was the unidentified victim a casualty of the infamous Italian Black Hand gangs? Others thought the victim was nothing more than unfortunate individual brought to Erie to be disposed of.

Nearly twenty-four hours after the discovery of the charred remains on Zimmerman Road, police had no answers for the public as to the identity of the unknown man—or why he was killed.

What was certain was that police believed the victim was transported to the scene by automobile. Marks in the ground and bloodstains indicated he was struck over the head while standing in the road, possibly restrained or distracted, and afterward his body was dragged into Blackwood's potato patch. There, the murderer, or murderers, took a two-quart water bottle full of gasoline and nearly emptied the contents onto the corpse. In an attempt to set the corpse ablaze and hasten the process of destroying the victim's identity, they might have burned themselves while taking a branch from a nearby sumac tree to stir the flames.

On the morning of August 16, 1920, the *Erie Daily Times* reported a possible break in the case. The body had been positively identified.

Angelo Desabio, a day clerk at the New Morton House on the corner of Fifteenth and Peach Streets, identified the body as that of Harold W. Smith of Hornell, New York, who had been rooming at the hotel since July 29. The identification instilled a newfound confidence in investigators as they sought to question Desabio and planned an examination of Smith's room at the Morton House.

Desabio told police Smith rented the room for a week. Smith, Desabio recalled, was not particularly well dressed. Upon searching Smith's room at the Morton House, police located an old pair of trousers, a nightshirt, several collars and a razor outfit in a package. Other additional items of clothing from Smith's room were taken to police headquarters that day.[153]

When viewing the body, Desabio was almost positive that the clothes matched what Smith was wearing the last time he saw him and claimed the features of the charred body appeared to match the basic contours of Smith's face. Smith had also not been seen for the three days prior to the discovery of the body.

Brugger's Undertaking Parlors had become besieged with endless inquiries from hundreds of individuals claiming to know the identity of the murdered man as well as the morbidly curious.[154] The *Erie Dispatch* threw cold water on

Birds Eye View Showing the Erie Depot, Erie, Pa.

Looking west toward Peach Street and the rear of the Morton House. *Author's collection.*

the *Times*'s break, claiming that the body had been unsuccessfully "positively identified" as four different men at Brugger's[155] and remained unidentified. Following up on numerous clues and tips to the man's possible identity left the police both perplexed and surprised at how many men were "missing" in the city at that time.

The *Times* also reported that it was possible that the police had located the murder car used in the crime, said to have been located in a local garage; however, other reports indicate the police stopped the vehicle at the corner of Seventeenth and State Streets without a license plate. It was rumored blood and clots of hair were found inside, but this was not confirmed by detectives, who were performing a search of the owner through the factory and engine numbers of the car.

Portions of the dead man's scalp along with clumps of hair were found alongside the roadway when police performed an additional search of the scene on Zimmerman Road. Detective August Heisler, in charge of the day squad of investigators, chalked the murder up as being the work of one of numerous characters within Erie's criminal underworld.[156] Although detectives differed on the motive, it was universally believed that the victim and his murderer, or murderers, were acquainted. District Attorney Charles Arthur Blass spent his time working alongside the police. Blass was confident that those responsible would be apprehended and the victim identified.

Hopes were dashed when, on August 17, Harold Smith was reported to be alive and well in Buffalo, having apparently fled from authorities in Detroit on a grand larceny charge. It would be the first of many embarrassing blunders as the police struggled to gain a foothold on a murder case that had already attracted attention of circus-like proportions.

With the investigation back to square one, police turned their focus on the victim and evidence, in the hopes an identification would lead to his killer. Although the victim was originally believed to be around twenty-one years of age, police were now certain that he was between the ages of thirty-five and forty. The boilermaker's hammer, nearly two feet in length, was the only other main piece of evidence besides the scorched water bottle. Other detectives set off into the streets and alleyways of Erie in search of clues. The investigation was hampered by numerous reports of persons reported missing as the days went on.

Employees of the Erie Lighting Company claimed a Polish co-worker matched the description of the body. But when detectives dug deeper, they found the supposed victim at home eating dinner.[157]

Despite dozens of people claiming to know the identity of the victim, acting coroner Theobald M. Flynn[158] notified police that unless the body was identified within twenty-four hours, it would be necessary to have it interred. Because Brugger's lacked the proper cooling methods to preserve the corpse, the internal gases inside the body had begun to distort the features, according to Flynn, resulting in early decomposition.[159]

Famed Erie County detective Frank H. Watson worked quietly behind the scenes with District Attorney Blass and the Erie City Police. Watson remarked that the fact that so many positive identifications had failed to materialize into tangible clues indicated the difficulty of identifying the dead man.[160] Calls continued to come in, with police continuing to allow plausible identifications to take place at Brugger's. By the afternoon of the seventeenth, three individuals had come forward believing they knew the identity of the victim. These identifications, too, were incorrect, and police found themselves at a dead end.

County Detective Watson, speaking to the *Times*, was one of the few who believed that the man was not killed on Zimmerman Road at all. The victim, Watson believed, had probably been beaten somewhere in the city, loaded inside the vehicle and taken to the spot where those responsible burned the remains to prevent further identification. This was at odds with most of the investigators, who believed the massive amounts of blood found in the road supported the theory that the victim was alive on Zimmerman Road.[161]

The case was dealt additional blows when automobiles found in the area at the time of the murder were determined to be unrelated and an attempt to trace the water bottle failed to locate the original owners. The investigation, however, continued, with the police searching all garages within the city, pointing to the theory that a garage fight preceded the murder. Taxicabs were also searched but failed to provide additional clues.

It was at this time that authorities had no choice but to offer a reward, which had already garnered support from acting coroner Flynn and District Attorney Blass, with Blass planning on approaching the county commissioners for a reward. "I am of the firm opinion that this would be the best way to get an early solution of the murder started,"[162] Flynn said.

To assist the authorities, the *Erie Dispatch* amended its description of the victim by the morning of August 18:

> *The man was 5 feet, 2 inches in height, weighed between 125 and 130 pounds, and was between 25 and 30 years of age, with jet black hair streaked with gray and a full set of natural teeth. At the time the body was discovered it was clad in grey trousers with black perpendicular stripes, grey socks, a cotton crepe shirt. No coat or cap was discovered. Tan shoes were found upon the feet and a common leather belt was around the waist. There were no distinguishable marks or scars upon the body.*[163]

Just as police appeared to have exhausted all leads, Detective Sergeants Liebel, Scalise and Patrolman Englert uncovered what would be their most promising lead yet. Following the discovery of the body on Zimmerman Road, individuals who lived around St. John Kanty Prep, located on Copper Mill Road, reported that the night prior a vehicle had been seen stopped in the vicinity. It was only later that a blood-soaked coat, with the sleeves inside out, was found in a gulley. Detective Sergeants Liebel, Scalise and Patrolman Englert quietly pursued their lead while the press and public were distracted by the endless carousel of false identifications.

Inside one of the coat pockets was a card from General Electric belonging to an Italian immigrant by the name of Joseph Bolla. General Electric foreman Harry Breecher oversaw Bolla in the Engine Cab Department and was taken to Brugger's and asked if he could make a positive identification of the remains. Breecher was unable to swear positively that it was Bolla but admitted that the general features and style of clothing matched.

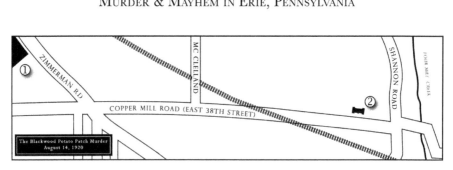

Map showing the location of (1) John Blackwood's farm and (2) where the bloodied coat was found discarded in a gully.

Bolla had been employed at General Electric, and with the assistance of fellow employees, it was revealed that he had been staying in Wesleyville. Bolla had not been seen for at least two weeks. Before disappearing, Bolla informed his bosses at General Electric that he was going to visit his sister in Chicago and did not care for the work at General Electric anymore. Authorities also learned that Bolla had possibly used the name Giuseppe Calafato. Police searched Bolla's lodgings and also revisited the similar murder of Joseph Scambera, an Erie man killed in Cleveland in 1919.[164] It remains unknown if there were any connecting pieces of evidence in both cases. It was at this point in the investigation that the possible identification of Joseph Bolla was leaked to the press.

The *Erie Daily Times* and the *Erie Dispatch* bombarded the police and District Attorney's Office about the supposed identification. *The Erie Daily Times* proclaimed on August 19, that the authorities felt certain that the dead man was Joseph Bolla. This conflicted with District Attorney Blass and County Detective Watson, who weren't talking and refused to confirm or deny the reports. This did nothing to deter the press, who claimed, "experts in crimes investigating the slaying here and that in Cleveland have all the earmarks of an Italian murder."[165]

Endless speculation and accompanying theories were fueled by the sensationalism on the front pages of the *Times* and the *Dispatch*, whose gory daily details provided the people of Erie with the murder and mayhem they craved. Acting coroner Flynn remained concerned about the condition of the body because of the progress of decomposition; he stated, "I do not think that the body will last longer than 24 hours, but it is up to the police to order internment."[166]

While District Attorney Blass pushed for a reward, County Detective Watson felt the bloody coat was the best clue. And several days into the investigation, seven detectives within the Erie Police Department were

The Erie City Police Department, circa 1918. *From the* Police Journal, *June 1918.*

working around the clock on the case. Blass and Watson continued to deny the body had been identified despite the continued leaks from those within the investigation who said otherwise.

The *Erie Daily Times* believed that the murder on Zimmerman Road was destined to go down in history along with other infamous unsolved murder cases such as that of Manley W. Keene, an investigation that the *Times* still believed was "muffed by the authorities."[167]

On August 22, 1920, the police acknowledged that the remains found in Blackwood's potato patch on August 14, 1920, were most likely that of Italian Joseph Bolla, who was still unaccounted for. Charles Brugger, of Brugger's Undertaking and Funeral Parlors, stated that the body had been embalmed and sealed in a copper casket. "Every attention has been given to the body," Brugger said, "and there has been little or no decomposition. Under instructions from police I have been forced to refuse many people the privilege of reviewing the body and will have to refuse others unless they are authorized by the police to review the remains."[168]

It was at this point in the investigation that records become murky about what occurred and who was questioned. What is known is that on August 24 the police informed reporters that the bloodied coat did not actually belong to Joseph Bolla and that the owner had been located—alive and well. County Detective Watson remarked to the *Erie Dispatch*, "I cannot turn over what information I have on hand so that it may become public property. But as soon as certain things have been accomplished I will give out a statement covering our activities from the day the murder was discovered."[169]

From that moment on, the case grew cold—at least for the next two weeks.

A COLD-BLOODED MURDER IN PLAIN VIEW

Forty-two-year-old fruit dealer Joseph Giammanco celebrated the christening of his two-month-old daughter, Josephine, on the afternoon of September 12, 1920. Later that night, Giammanco held a celebration at his residence, 1519 Chestnut Street, in a garage at the rear of the home. Over one hundred men, women and children were in attendance, partaking in various Italian dishes, listening to music and dancing. Around 11:45 p.m., the joyful atmosphere was shattered by a rapid succession of gunshots. The noise ceased as guests drifted toward the front of Giammanco's house. Others were so terrified by the gunshots that they "remained seated about the garage as if nailed to their seats."[170]

An unidentified nine-year-old girl found twenty-nine-year-old Louie Romano, an Italian auto salesman, lying crumpled on the front lawn. Soon a crowd gathered in the yard, and phone calls trickled into police headquarters. Within minutes, all available detectives and officers converged upon the scene. Other guests rang the home of Dr. Samuel Scibetta, several blocks away. Scibetta arrived within minutes and found Romano's body on the lawn, "lying in a composed position with the legs crossed and the arms lying by the sides of the body."[171]

With the area secured just past midnight, around fifteen detectives and officers started questioning witnesses. Soon Erie County coroner Cassius M. Cardot arrived on scene and ordered the body removed to Brugger's Undertaking & Funeral Parlors for further examination and an autopsy.

As hard as the police hit the ground running in search of clues, they found very little. Those in attendance did not say much, if anything to the police. Rumors were whispered about the possible involvement of the Black Hand gang, but this was unconfirmed. What was known about Romano was that he had been in Erie about four months. Giammanco told police that Romano often conducted a small auto repair business in the garage behind the residence.[172]

Despite some of the guests converging on the scene within seconds, nobody was able to provide any tangible information about what had actually occurred. All that was known was that just prior to 11:45 p.m., Louie Romano walked to the front of Giammanco's residence, where he was shot by a person or persons unknown.

The early morning hours of September 13 turned up little in terms of evidence of the shooting, with the only viable clue being a theft of a Ford vehicle, stolen from 1250 East Twenty-Second Street, and even this was

Present-day photograph showing the northeast corner of Chestnut and West Sixteenth Street where the Giammanco residence once stood. *Author's collection.*

far from certain as being connected to the shooting. Some items found on Romano led police to the rooming house of Mabel Cleveland, 1721 Chestnut Street. It was there, police learned, that Romano had been a boarder for the past month; he was said to be quiet and little was known about his life and background. Mabel Cleveland attested that Romano had been out of town for a week and returned to Erie only four days prior to his death.

In Romano's room, police located a .38 revolver in the drawer of a bureau. A letter, written in Italian, was also discovered,[173] along with a book; the name of a woman inscribed on the inside jacket appeared to have an Ohio address. Coroner Cardot briefly examined Romano's body and discovered that he had been shot five times at close range, most of which were around his heart, with at least one bullet passing through the heart directly[174] and two of the bullets entering the right side of the chest. Cardot believed that any one of the first four shots were sufficient to render death instantly to the victim.[175]

Morning rumors in Erie's Little Italy neighborhood spread that Louie Romano met his death at the hands of a jealous rival. Other rumors spurred from the sensational belief that the Black Hand had infiltrated the Italian community. Police searched throughout the neighborhood but found no

Erie County coroner Dr. Cassius M. Cardot. *From the* Erie Daily Times.

evidence to support such theories, all while those in Little Italy looked on in silence.

That morning, coroner Cardot announced an autopsy would be performed as soon as possible. District Attorney Blass expressed the possibility that the murder of Romano and the case of Joseph Bolla were likely committed by the same gang or organization. When pressed further, Blass refused to comment,[176] although his earlier comments were supported by a substantial amount of evidence that connected the murders of Bolla and Romano, something that remained hidden from the public.

This evidence included the fact that Louie Romano was actually Anthony Sperandeo, formerly of 2713 Dennison Avenue, Cleveland, and prior to his death he had been under surveillance by the police department in Erie, suspected of being a part of an automobile thieving ring. Although he was known to those in Erie's Little Italy as Louie Romano, Sperandeo had a history of utilizing various aliases.[177]

Police also discovered the Ford automobile stolen from 1250 East Twenty-Second Street had been recovered in Rochester, New York. William Roucher and Orval Reissinger were arrested and charged with stealing the vehicle. Police investigated the auto theft and cleared Roucher and Reissinger of involvement in the Sperandeo and Bolla murders, and they were extradited to Erie and found guilty of breaking and entering and larceny of an automobile.

The autopsy of Anthony Sperandeo confirmed that he had been shot not five but twelve times.[178] Bullet holes and powder burns were found on his front and back, indicating he had been shot by two gunmen at close range. Sperandeo's brother-in-law Sam Marcelino and a nephew, Dominick Dimanuro, arrived from Cleveland and confirmed Sperandeo's identity .

Meanwhile, a closer examination by police into Sperandeo's personal belongings confirmed he had dealt in stolen automobiles, the majority of which were brought through Erie so that they could be changed and disguised to prevent identification by falsifying the vendor certificates. Sperandeo would then fence the automobiles to other cities such as Buffalo, Rochester, Toledo, Cleveland and Detroit—even Canada.[179] Police also felt this was a factor in his death.

Police learned Sperandeo had kept automobiles at Fidelity Garage located at 363 West Eighteenth Street. It was here that Sperandeo sold an automobile to one of the owners of the garage, Clyde Morgan. When Morgan learned the car had been stolen, he returned the vehicle to the original owner and demanded a refund. Sperandeo refunded Morgan's money and then moved his business from Morgan's garage. For police, however, the biggest hurdle in the Sperandeo investigation was Little Italy itself.

It was around 1864 that the first Italian immigrants settled in Erie, Pennsylvania. By 1895, Erie's Italian population had grown and consisted of four settlements within the city, with Little Italy being the largest of them. Located on West Sixteenth Street between Cherry and Poplar Streets, bordered by West Sixteenth and Walnut Streets, the population within the settlement of nine city blocks had grown to three thousand by 1911. At the heart of Little Italy was the city's first Italian church, St. Paul's Roman Catholic Church.

In many respects, Little Italy operated much like its own city. It had two banks, the Bank of Italy and the Italian American Bank, and its own newspapers, *La Progresso* and *La Fiamma*. Local Italian doctors founded the Rose Memorial Hospital, and many locals were members of social organizations such as the La Nuova Aurora Society and Calabrese Club. Little Italy was notorious among the Erie City Police Department for being an area that could make criminal investigations difficult, with witnesses willing to speak few and far between.

As darkness crept through the neighborhood on September 13, 1920, District Attorney Blass led a squad of detectives through Little Italy in yet another additional sweep. Others questioned Sperandeo's brother-in-law, curious about how he learned of Sperandeo's death so quickly. Marcelino told police that he had been called at the market and was told he was needed at home. At home, he found his wife grief-stricken over the news, which was reportedly delivered from an unknown individual.

Hope that Sperandeo's murderer or murderers would be captured was strengthened with additional testimony from witnesses who came forward. Lawrence Songer, 1528 Chestnut Street, lived across from where the murder occurred.

Erie County District Attorney C. Arthur Blass. *By Gary Dombrowski.*

Sitting on the veranda of his home before the murder took place, Songer saw a Ford touring car pull up in front of the Giammanco home. Four men wearing straw hats exited the vehicle and engaged in a discussion. Songer then went inside his home, and a few minutes he later heard gunshots fired in rapid succession. When Songer exited to investigate, the Ford touring car and men had vanished.

Two other witnesses, Fred Fisher and Rufus Horrel, New York Central Railroad employees, were walking on Chestnut Street when Sperandeo was shot on the opposite side of the street by two men, small of stature and wearing caps. When the firing ceased, both men ran into a vacant lot north of 1501 Chestnut Street and vanished. The witnesses, although slightly conflicting, were considered important by police. Police also questioned Joseph Giammanco in regard to his relationship with Sperandeo. Giammanco denied that those responsible for killing Sperandeo were guests at his party and was unable to assist the police further.

On September 14, Sam Marcelino and Dominick Dimanuro left Erie with Sperandeo's remains. After arriving in Cleveland, Sperandeo's body was laid out at 3717 Dennison Avenue before being buried on September 16, 1920, in Cavalry Cemetery in Cleveland, Ohio.

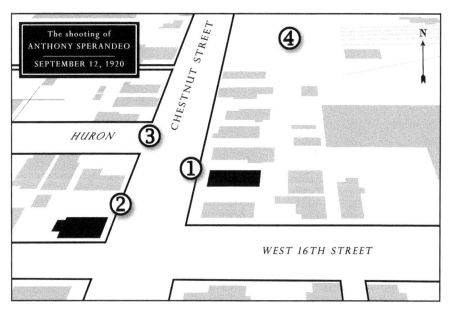

Map showing the (1) Giammanco residence, (2) Lawrence Songer, (3) Rufus Horrel and Fred Fisher and (4) the vacant lot where the gunman disappeared.

Sperandeo's murder opened the floodgates to a wealth of information that allowed police to not only track the secret numbers for hundreds of vehicles fenced through operations of the Erie auto thieves but also uncovered operations preceding the murder several months prior. By September 16, police had located twenty-eight stolen cars in Rochester connected to Sperandeo's operations in Erie.[180]

One thing that puzzled investigators was that Sperandeo was said to have had more than $1,000 in his possession and had been seen with a large sum of money prior to his death. Only a single dollar bill and some loose change were found on Sperandeo's body. This suggested a possible motive for robbery. On September 15, 1920, police confirmed a connection between the murder of Joseph Bolla and Anthony Sperandeo and announced they were following up on additional clues. But what these clues were remains unknown.

The gang operation evidence, although rewarding, still presented concerns to the police. In addition to dealing with Prohibition, there was only so much the Erie City Police Department and those of nearby cities could provide in terms of manpower and attention to evidence. Detectives had reached out to other cities with lists of acquaintances and friends of Sperandeo and asked those departments to look into their backgrounds and whereabouts.

Police learned from several individuals that Sperandeo had left Erie ten days before his death. He returned just four days prior to his death. Police were certain that Sperandeo's four last days in Erie certainly were connected to his death but lacked definitive proof. Friends of Sperandeo, seen in his company before the murder, had disappeared, and those in the Italian community remained silent.

The inquest into Sperandeo's murder was held on September 17, 1920, at Brugger's Undertaking & Funeral Parlor with Coroner Cardot presiding. Four witnesses—Fred Fisher, Rufus Horrel, Joseph Giammanco and Lawrence Songer—presented testimony before the jury. Fisher, Horrel and Songer reiterated information already presented to police, and special attention then was turned to Giammanco.

Giammanco confirmed Sperandeo rented his barn, using it as a garage. At first, Giammanco knew Sperandeo as Louie Romano but later learned his real identity. When Giammanco learned that Sperandeo sold a stolen car, he asked Sperandeo to vacate his premises. Sperandeo then moved his operation of business to a location on West Eighteenth Street. Giammanco admitted he knew of the auto thieving gang of which Sperandeo was a member. "I'm afraid of them," Giammanco said. "They come there and killed that man and they would do the same thing to me if they were given the chance. I knew that man was not Louis Romano but I did not want to get mixed in their affairs."[181]

The jury returned a verdict that the Erie City Police Department had become all too familiar with: "By murderous intent by a person or persons at present unknown."

District Attorney Blass assured the public that everything was being done to capture the men responsible for Sperandeo's murder.[182]

As more stolen automobiles were recovered, police were assisted by a special investigator from the Great American Indemnity company of Mansfield, Ohio. The number of vehicles had grown to such an extent that Detective Sergeants Heisler and Sandusky and Motorcycle Officer Carl Althof were assigned to separately search for the stolen cars and focus on their recovery to their original owners.[183]

Through careful examination it was learned that a unique white-wheeled Ford touring car—similar to one seen at the scene of the torch murder of Joseph Bolla—passed through Sperandeo's hands around August. And as the investigation into the auto theft ring progressed, so did the investigation into the murder of Joseph Bolla. It was through this investigation that police kept circling back to the individual who had owned the Ford touring car. His name appeared in paperwork found in Sperandeo's room, and he was also the owner of the bloody coat with Bolla's identification card: Joseph Calafato.

OMERTÀ

After Anthony Sperandeo's body was pumped full of lead, police were drawn to a name that they had uncovered during the investigation into the Blackwood potato patch murder.

When Joseph Bolla was tentatively identified as the body found in Blackwood's potato patch, police were originally of the opinion Bolla had used the alias Giuseppe or Joseph Calafato. Although it is not clear how this connection was made, it was likely due to an item or identifying marker on the bloodied coat that was turned over to police. Police eventually located Joseph Calafato, who was alive and well in Buffalo, New York. Other additional information seems to have pointed to Calafato and after Sperandeo was murder, Erie police again found themselves speaking with Calafato when

An older Joseph Calafato smiles for his mug shot. *From the* Erie Daily Times.

he was proven to be a known acquaintance of Sperandeo. Police also believed he knew Joseph Bolla, too. Police also confirmed Calafato owned a Ford touring car with white wheels—identical to the vehicle spotted on Zimmerman Road the night of Bolla's murder.

In October 1920, Joseph Calafato was arrested in Buffalo, New York, for involvement in an auto theft. Calafato was ultimately released when he was able to produce a bill of sale. Things appeared to have calmed down for some time—that is, until Calafato was arrested again on May 23, 1921. He was found in possession of a stolen automobile out of Cleveland, Ohio; charged by the federal government with an interstate violation; and held on $10,000 bail and a trial date set for September.

Several weeks prior to his questioning by Erie authorities, Calafato was again arrested by Buffalo authorities when he and another man, Frank Dimato, were charged with larceny of a machine owned by a former Buffalo police officer. Calafato, it was said, was alleged to have stolen and sold the car. He was subsequently charged in Erie County Court and released on $5,000 bail.

While Calafato was held in Buffalo, he received a visit on July 19, 1921, from District Attorney Blass, County Detective Edward Wagner and Detective Louis Scalise. The men interviewed Calafato, advising him that they were interested in questioning him in regard to a series of automobile theft cases in Erie County. Authorities asked Calafato if he would be willing to return to Erie and answer additional questions about the cases. Calafato agreed, and the men drove back, arriving in Erie later that night.

On the morning of July 20, 1921, Calafato was taken to the office of Police Chief William Detzel and grilled for about an hour by Chief Detzel, District Attorney Blass and Detective Scalise. When pressed about the murder of Joseph Bolla, Calafato denied that he owned a Ford touring vehicle similar to the one seen near the crime scene. It was only when Scalise provided paperwork proving Calafato owned the vehicle that he finally confessed that he was, in fact, the owner of the vehicle.

Police also provided evidence Bolla and Calafato rented a garage in the city the summer prior to Bolla's death. Calafato reluctantly admitted this as well and went so far as to acknowledge that Bolla had given him the money to pay the first month's rent for the garage.[184] By this point in the investigation, police had come to realize that Calafato—not Sperandeo—was the brains of the auto thieving organization, and there was a reason why he was known as "The Fox."

Giuseppe Calafato was born on March 22, 1898, in the commune of Ravanusa, Sicily, to Giuseppe and Lena Calafato. Scant information is known about his life before immigrating to America in September 1913 aboard the SS *Chicago*, which departed from Le Havre, France, where his sister resided. The earliest Calafato is mentioned in records appears when World War I registration records list him residing at 611½ West Sixteenth Street in Erie, Pennsylvania, employed at the Griffin Manufacturing Company on Cherry Street.[185]

The arrival of Prohibition created endless opportunities for those seeking to circumvent the law and become involved in bootlegging alcohol. Throughout 1920 until Prohibition's end in 1933, crime skyrocketed not only in Erie but throughout the entire country. It was believed that Giuseppe Calafato was widely involved in the bootlegging business of his uncle Louis Calafato out of Cleveland, Ohio.

By August 1920, Calafato had become involved in the auto thieving ring with Bolla, the two of them operating a garage together. Both men were also working with Sperandeo, with Calafato overseeing operations through Buffalo and Cleveland. It was believed that before his death, Bolla quarreled with Calafato and Sperandeo about money. With the dispute creating risks he did not want—or need—Calafato lured Bolla into his vehicle and either murdered him or had someone else dispose of him in the potato patch on Zimmerman Road.

Bolla's death, in turn, was believed to have led to a quarrel between Calafato and Sperandeo. Perhaps Sperandeo threatened Calafato's life, and in retaliation before he could strike, Calafato had him snubbed out. Fearing two murders within the span of two weeks would bring heat on him and the auto thieving business, Calafato fled the city.[186]

Calafato denied involvement in either of the murders, only admitting that he knew Bolla longer than Sperandeo. Calafato claimed that he left Erie on August 11, three days before Bolla's murder, and heard about his death while in Cleveland. Grilled again the following day, Calafato retracted his prior statements about Bolla and Sperandeo and denied all knowledge of the crime. District Attorney Blass revealed evidence that showed that Bolla was from Ravanusa, Sicily, and arrived in America at the same time as Calafato.

Calafato also disputed the paperwork showing he owned the Ford touring car, claiming Sperandeo owned it.[187]

As for the $17,000 used to post bail for recent charges in Buffalo, Blass asked Calafato how he obtained that much money.

"Stole it," Calafato grinned.

"Yes, you steal and kill both," District Attorney Blass snapped back.

Calafato grinned again with a shrug. "Sure, me kill, kill ten thousand people."[188]

It was clear Calafato viewed the interrogation as a cat-and-mouse game. There were times during questioning when Calafato would nod in response, pretending not to understand English, only to later speak proficiently. This led detectives to believe he understood without the need of an interpreter. Building a circumstantial case against Calafato was one thing. Proving that he physically murdered Bolla and Sperandeo was something different.

Calafato was subjected to a third straight day of grilling before Chief Detzel on July 22, 1921, and continued to deny his involvement in the murders of Sperandeo and Bolla. Locals from the Italian neighborhood were also brought to police headquarters in an attempt to confirm Calafato was seen with Bolla before his death. Calafato, who remained tight-lipped, was asked why he wouldn't talk.

"I don't dare squeal," Calafato responded. "If I do, I get killed and also my pal. If I don't talk I got a chance to get out."[189]

Calafato was not your typical run-of-the-mill criminal. He was smart and knew the law. He also knew that by not talking he almost guaranteed his way to freedom—saving his own skin at his own expense. After Calafato was taken back to his cell, his attorney, Sam Rossiter, went before Judge William E. Hirt to obtain a writ of habeas corpus. Rossiter, the *Times* claimed, gained Calafato as a client due to the financial assistance of an "organized gang of auto thieves,"[190] which supported the belief that Calafato was the leader of the gang in Erie.

In a hearing before Judge Hirt, Rossiter claimed Calafato was arrested and committed to jail on a blank warrant and that a charge of murder against his client was not unveiled until the day before. Rossiter also attacked Blass's decision to rearraign Calafato before Alderman Hayes and prepare a new warrant. Judge Hirt denied the habeas corpus request and remanded Calafato to be held at the county jail without bail. District Attorney Blass, meanwhile, charged Calafato with the just the murder of Joseph Bolla based on fact that the circumstantial evidence was stronger in Bolla's murder.

Detective Sergeant Louis Scalise. *By Gary Dombrowski.*

Blass had begun to prepare for the trial against Calafato. However, when he appeared before Alderman Hayes on the morning of September 6, 1921, District Attorney Blass, who had prepared to proceed with a preliminary hearing with twenty-six witnesses ready to testify, asked Alderman Hayes to release Calafato.

District Attorney Blass's request shocked the public. Blass, however, appears to have made a careful decision. He stated that instead of revealing the evidence against Calafato, he would rather have Calafato released and wait for additional evidence, sought by Detective Scalise, to secure a conviction. Blass justified his reasoning, "If I should take Califato into court now with the circumstantial evidence I have and it should result in his release we would never be able to try him on the same charges in the courts of Erie County."[191]

Although charges were dropped against Calafato for the Bolla murder, he was immediately shadowed by the Erie City Police and authorities in Buffalo for quite some time afterward. Toward the end of March 1923, Erie City Police notified Buffalo authorities that Calafato was on his way to Buffalo. On March 25, 1923, while visiting friends on Trenton Avenue, Calafato had been tipped off that Buffalo police were looking for him. When two officers attempted to speak with him, he fled and was caught with a loaded pistol in his possession.[192]

When questioned by police, Calafato again refused to talk. At the same time of Calafato's arrest, police in Cleveland raided a boardinghouse and found thousands of dollars in stolen automobile parts and accessories. The raid was made with cooperation from both Erie and Buffalo authorities.[193] An inspection of the stolen parts revealed that the auto thieving gang was still at work, stealing parts from vehicles in Buffalo and disposing of them in Cleveland.

Calafato was charged and released and does not appear to have done any prison time. On July 30, 1923, Calafato married Antonina "Lena" Altadonna, daughter of Salvatore and Theresa Amato. Salvatore Altadonna was none other than Joseph Giammanco.[194]

During the four-year tenure under District Attorney Charles Arthur Blass, Erie saw twenty-four murders, with the Bolla and Sperandeo murders being two of eight unsolved cases.[195] After M. Levant Davis succeeded Blass as district attorney in January 1924, Blass returned to private practice. From 1945 to 1961, Blass was a state senator and briefly served as the president of the Erie County Bar Association from 1951 to 1952. Blass died on November 14, 1970, at his residence in Millcreek Township.

Following Calafato's release, the murders of Anthony Sperandeo and Joseph Bolla slipped into the collection of unsolved murder investigations in the files of the Erie County District Attorney's office. But the case would receive attention again in 1924 when another burned corpse was found in nearby Crawford County.

A RAGING INFERNO IN THE DEAD OF NIGHT

It was around 7:30 a.m. on May 3, 1924, when trails of smoke billowed out of a barn on the property of Samuel Wiley in Sugar Grove Township, sixty miles south of Erie. A morning mist clung to the wheat fields that stretched into the nearby woodlots. Wiley had woken up around 1:40 that morning to find his barn engulfed in flames. The barn, which had fallen into disrepair and housed only some old hay and straw, was beyond saving. Wiley watched the fire, making sure it did not spread to any of the other buildings on his property. When the fire died down, Wiley went back to bed and planned on inspecting the damage later that morning.

Passing through the fields near the barn, Wiley found a discarded cap on the ground and noticed that it was bloodstained. An imprint showed it was manufactured by the Smith Brothers, a haberdasher shop in Meadville. Calling to a farmhand, James Barry, both men continued inspecting the field and discovered signs that something had been dragged through the field and across the road. The trail continued in the direction of the still smoking remains of the barn. The men's stomachs dropped when they noticed bloodstains in the road.

When Wiley and Berry inspected the barn, they made a gruesome discovery: the remains of a body, burned beyond recognition, the legs, arms and head missing. At first, the men thought it looked to be that of what used to be a woman, but they weren't so sure. Nearby, a silver belt buckle was found with some keys, a plain silver ring and some coins. A discarded five-gallon gasoline can was also found.[196] Both men rushed to contact the authorities.

Coroner William McGrath from Sharon arrived with Deputy Coroner Preston Steele and detectives. Although it appears the autopsy—if one was performed—has not survived, there is input from W.S. Morrow, who was working near the crime scene. Morrow had worked as a farmer and mill worker and had experience in recovering dead bodies. Morrow inspected the remains:

> *I determined on the stab wounds because after the remains of the murdered man were found by us in the ashes of the fire early Friday morning, certainly inside of a few hours, I bent down over the partially burned body and found two wounds, one in the base of the neck under the chin and another in the chest. Blood was oozing out of both openings. The flesh was partially burned off. When I pressed my finger over each opening I brought to the surface a drop of blood.*[197]

An inquest was held and, despite few facts, brought before a jury, who determined that an unknown individual had come to his/her death at the hands of a person or persons unknown. Later that day, the charred remains were interred in the Shenango Valley Cemetery in Greenville, Pennsylvania.

When news of the discovered corpse in Greenville reached Erie, the *Times* immediately sent a reporter to the Wiley farm to investigate and gather additional information.[198]

The investigation was led by Pennsylvania State Police corporal John J. Broski from the Butler Barracks with assistance from Lawrence Park Barracks of Erie County. Corporal Broski and state police focused on the cap from Meadville. This gave the police the only clue they had to the identity of the unknown victim.

Further investigation at the Wiley farm found sets of footprints, said to be a size six and a half men's shoe. Also found were remnants of the victim's clothing, charred, burned and soaked in oil. The *Times* described the clothing recovered:

> *Further examination of the remains of the body disclosed a fragment of the shirt, collar and tie, the man had worn. The small trademark at the back of the collar showed the shirt to have been a "Treymore" and was of cream silk material with red stripes. It was undoubtedly a "loud" shirt. The collar was detachable, of soft linen and the fragment of tie that remained showed that it was course knit fabric, of the latest design. These items point to the supposition that the man was quite well dressed, but furthermore, the oil stained fragments show that the whole body had been saturated with kerosene to assure its burning.*[199]

A witness, J.M. Denison of Jamestown, Pennsylvania, informed authorities that he had happened to drive past the barn on the night it was set ablaze and saw an automobile on the side of the roadway.[200]

While the investigation centered on Meadville, police already had an idea about the identity of the victim and were sure that he was a local Italian from Erie involved in bootlegging, something police believed was connected to his death. The key that was also found near the body, believed to be to a P.O. box, turned out to be a key to a Nash automobile. The number on the key allowed authorities to reach out to the Nash Motor Company in Wisconsin in an attempt to track down the owner.

The torch murder from Greenville had all the hallmarks of the murder of Joseph Bolla in 1920. Erie City Police were sure that it was possible that the work was of the same individuals—and they were proven correct when Pennsylvania State Police shifted their investigation to Erie a day later. Just like the Bolla murder, neighbors around the crime scene in Greenville reported to authorities that they heard no noises that night. And just like the Bolla murder, there were few initial clues that pointed to those responsible.

On the afternoon of May 7, 1924, state police authorities confirmed the victim was Tony "Lean Wolf" Chiappiloni. Police also located Chiappiloni's vehicle in a garage on Park Avenue in Meadville and, upon twisting the key in the ignition, confirmed their suspicions were correct when the vehicle roared to life. Witnesses reported Chiappiloni had last been seen leaving the car in the garage on May 2, 1924—the night of his murder.

Chiappiloni's death was also chalked up as being the result of a local bootlegging war. Unlike the Bolla investigation, Chiappiloni's body was quickly interred. This was also likely due to the fact that the remains were damaged to such an extent that a positive identification would be impossible.

Mary Mariano, held at the Crawford County jail for liquor law violations, was one of the last individuals known to have seen Chiappiloni alive. She said she had talked with him around 6:00 p.m. the day before the body was found and that he called on her regularly. Chiappiloni told Mary that he would visit her again the following day, around 10:30 a.m. He never showed.

Police in Erie knew Chiappiloni by his alias Tony Mariano. He was well known within local bootlegging circles throughout Erie, Venango, Mercer and Crawford

Murder suspect and victim Tony Chiappiloni. *From the Erie Daily Times.*

Counties, although he had never actually been arrested for any liquor law violations. "The dead man was undoubtedly Tony Chiappaloni. And Tony has undoubtedly been given a taste of his own medicine," remarked one of the officials from the Erie City Police Department. "Chiappaloni undoubtedly had a hand in if he did not instigate the 'bumping off' of Joe Botta."[201]

Erie police were also familiar with Chiappaloni due to his connection to the Bolla and Sperandeo murders and the auto thieving. They revealed to the *Times* that when Calafato was being shadowed by authorities in Buffalo, Chiappaloni was simultaneously being shadowed by the police in Erie.

When the case against Calafato was unable to proceed due to a lack of evidence, Chiappaloni remained in Erie until 1922, when he relocated to Meadville. He was arrested on November 1, 1923, by Detectives Scalise and Holtz on a charge of carrying a concealed weapon, a knife with a four-inch-long blade. When arraigned before an alderman, however, he was discharged. The last interaction police had with Chiappaloni was on March 9, 1924, during a raid on Peter Boni's pool room at 624 West Eighteenth Street. Boni, Chiappaloni (who used an alias) and five others were arrested, arraigned in court and fined two dollars and costs.[202]

Police questioned Mary Mariano further but were met with dead ends. Like the murders in Erie, the investigation into Chiappaloni's death never reached a conclusion, and it has since remained a mystery.

Much of Joseph Bolla's life remains unknown. Further attempts to locate any potential family and/or genealogical history are hampered by conflicting information from news reports and sources. Although he was never conclusively identified, the remains were buried under Bolla's name at the Old Almshouse Cemetery in Fairview, Pennsylvania. His murder, along with those of Anthony Sperandeo and Tony Chiappiloni, will likely remain unsolved.

Joseph Calafato would remain a presence in Erie's criminal underworld for decades to come. Calafato was present for—and briefly considered a suspect in—the murder of Dominick Brigilia on November 27, 1923. Brigilia was shot to death in a pool room owned by Frank "Scabouch" Arcar at 426 West Sixteenth Street.[203] When Calafato was arrested and quizzed by Erie City Police in the Brigilia investigation, it was revealed that he was wanted on a first-degree larceny charge out of Buffalo. Calafato was sent to Buffalo and held on the larceny charge, only to procure bail, thanks in part to his father-in-law, Joseph Giammanco.

Calafato, his father-in-law and another man were arrested in Ashtabula on December 7, 1923, when authorities located a shipment of stills in a truck driven by Calafato and Giammanco.[204]

In April 1925, in Conneaut, Ohio, authorities patrolled the countryside in an attempt to crack down on bootlegging. They came across a Hudson coach car acting strange and gave chase. After a considerable chase ensued, the car stopped and was abandoned by an unknown man clutching a gun. An inspection of the abandoned automobile revealed it was carrying wine and was registered to none other than Joseph Calafato. Calafato claimed that he lent the vehicle and denied being the driver.

In August 1927, the assassination of Louis Calafato,[205] Joseph's bootlegging uncle, in Cleveland, also called attention to the younger Calafato's activities in Erie.[206] The killing was said to have been the result of an ongoing bootlegging war between factions in Erie and Cleveland, and Cleveland authorities requested assistance from Erie City Police. It was known that the Calafato family operated stills somewhere in Erie County and distributed the liquor in both Cleveland and Buffalo.

With the death of Prohibition in 1933, Calafato's activities associated with bootlegging caught up with him when he was sued by the IRS in January 1938 for failure to pay his income tax assessment.[207] Calafato was later arrested and charged that following September for violations of Internal Revenue Service laws in relation to the seizure of an alcohol distillery on the E.M. Weaver Farm in North East.[208] Further disputes with the IRS over taxes would follow Calafato for the rest of his life.

Ensuing decades saw Calafato in charge of a numbers syndicate in Erie, and he was charged in 1940 for attempting to bribe an Erie City Police officer during the department's push to combat criminal activity. Calafato later admitted the bribe, was fined $750 and ordered to two years' probation. He served a six-month term in the Allegheny Workhouse when he violated the conditions of his probation. Calafato had not just dabbled in minor crimes since the 1920s as the press and others believed. This was apparent when Calafato was implicated in 1951 as part of an interstate crime ring with the release of the findings of the Kefauver Committee.[209] Calafato, it was said, had risen high up within Buffalo crime operations.

In 1951, the release of the Kefauver Committee findings, along with increased operations from the Erie City Police, resulted in a 70 percent reduction in gambling that year.[210] But the heat brought on by the federal government and the local police did nothing to deter Calafato when the Beaver Club, at the corner of Twelfth and State Streets, was raided in 1955. Calafato, then sixty years old, continued to engage in gambling operations until his death in July 1967 at the age of sixty-nine.

Detective Louis Scalise's role in the Bolla and Sperandeo homicides and the auto theft ring investigation highlighted some of his best work and demonstrated his ability to work within the community of Erie's Little Italy. Scalise would go on to close cases and lend his experience with the Italian community until December 30, 1937,[211] when in the early morning hours he was shot and killed by his son, Ralph, at their home. Louis Scalise was fifty-four years old.

It is almost assured that the murderers of Joseph Bolla, Anthony Sperandeo and Tony Chiappiloni will never be brought to justice. The case files have not survived; however, it is certainly clear from the police and press at the time that the murders were all connected to an interstate crime ring that stretched from Rochester, New York, all the way to the shores of Detroit, Michigan, with the help and assistance of crime factions that operated throughout the Great Lakes into the 1950s.

The Blackwood potato patch where Joseph Bolla's charred corpse was found no longer exists, with the Pennsylvania & Erie Railroad woods and property being long gone replaced by residential housing on Erie's east side. A baseball field sits on the site of Blackwood's potato patch.

Present-day location of Blackwood's potato patch. Joseph Bolla's body would have been located just to the left of the sidewalk. *Author's collection.*

Little Italy, where Anthony Sperandeo was murdered, still exists, although the Italian population has dwindled since the 1920s. The Italian newspapers have ceased publication for quite some time, and the once busy thoroughfare of various storefronts and restaurants on West 18th has long vanished. St. Paul's Roman Catholic Church remains one of the focal points of the neighborhood and, despite setbacks, is still going strong with what is left of Erie's Italian community.

The home of Salvatore Joseph Giammanco is gone, a victim to the ever-changing landscape, although one can still stand on the spot where Antonio Sperandeo's body was pumped full of lead on that still mysterious September night in 1920.

6

"EVERYWHERE THERE WAS BLOOD, BLOOD, BLOOD"

The Unsolved Murder of Rachel Levin

The morning of January 22, 1925, offered a brief respite for the citizens of Erie from the nagging winter cold that had plagued them for the last several weeks. Temperatures were slightly warmer but not warm enough to melt the snow that clung to the houses and ground surrounding the Nickel Plate Railroad tracks by French Street.

It was around 8:00 a.m. when a switchman spotted a grisly sight—a body lying in a ravine south of the tracks near the railroad bridge that crossed French Street. He immediately rushed to notify police of the discovery.

Detective Sergeants David Doyle and Julius Talbert were called to the crime scene and arrived there around 8:30 a.m., along with County Detective Leroy Search.

The *Times* reported, "Everywhere there was blood, blood, blood."[212]

The body of a woman was found lying in a northwest by southeast position, one of her shoes found nearby. The fur collar from her coat had been ripped, the coat itself slightly removed from the body. Around the body, roughly ten feet in diameter, snow, stained crimson, had been trampled down. Tracks in the snow indicated a struggle had taken place between the dead woman and her killer. Detectives inspected sets of footprints and determined they belonged to the victim and her killer. Sled tracks were found nearby, accompanied by smaller shoe prints that belonged to children who used the ravine for sledding.

Police also found a pair of man's brown woolen gloves and two handkerchiefs with the letter *P* embroidered on the corner. Erie County

Scene of Killing in Plain View
of a Passerby on French Street

The murder scene the following day. *From the* Erie Daily Times.

coroner Daniel Hanley arrived shortly after the call came into headquarters and performed an initial inspection of the body and determined she had not been dead long. Her face was frightfully beaten about, and it was only when her body was lifted from the ground that he located a ten-dollar bill.[213] By then, a curious crowd of onlookers and locals from the nearby Jewish neighborhoods had begun to cluster on the sidewalk.

Hanley had the unknown woman removed to his undertaking parlors. More officers arrived on the scene and began combing for additional clues throughout the area. The closest house was no more than seventy-five feet from the scene of the murder, and when questioned by police, Hattie Augstell of 1911 State street, recalled hearing the sound of something from behind her house around 9:00 p.m. "My brother, Edward, who is a barber at the Star Barber shop, had left the house but a short time when I heard this stumbling or dragging noise," Augstell told a *Times* reporter. "The sound was unusual and I went to the front of the house. I saw nothing."[214]

Clara Platt of 1916 French Street passed the scene of the murder about 11:30 p.m. on her way home and saw nothing out of the ordinary. Remarkably, two hundred feet to the south of the crime scene was the Erie County Milk Association. Between the hours of 2:00 to 6:00 a.m., roughly forty drivers entered and exited the plant. None of them recalled seeing anything alarming.

Evidence yielded no clues about the killer's identity to Detectives Doyle and Talbert. They believed the woman was attacked and murdered on the spot. This was evident due to the shoe tracks and activity around where the body was found. There was an absence of blood trail and markings, indicating she was not dragged or carried to that location. Whoever murdered the woman, police believed, would have been covered with blood.

Clara Smelowitz, 2207 French Street, stopped at the shop of tailor Charles Levin, located at 32 East Twenty-First Street. Just the day before, Charles's wife, Rachel, had visited Smelowitz and her family. Around 1:30 a.m., Charles had visited the Smelowitz family home, telling them Rachel was missing. As Charles labored about his dingy lodgings, he confirmed Rachel had still not returned home. Smelowitz told Levin to seek the aid of the police. Perhaps she had stayed with one of the numerous Jewish families in the nearby area? Within a short time, Clara Smelowitz left Levin's shop, and her attention was attracted to a small group of people still milling around the blood-covered snow.

Smelowitz left for Hanley's Undertaking Parlor and, along with several other Jewish men and women from the neighborhood, would identify the dead women as none other than Rachel Levin.

She was just twenty-seven years old.

As rumors spread through the city, reporters caught wind of the identification and headed for Levin's shop. Around 11:00 a.m. they notified Levin his wife had been found badly beaten near the ravine beyond his shop. Levin rushed to the scene and stood where her body had been. He surveyed the scene, taking in the surroundings, and inquired how she was found.

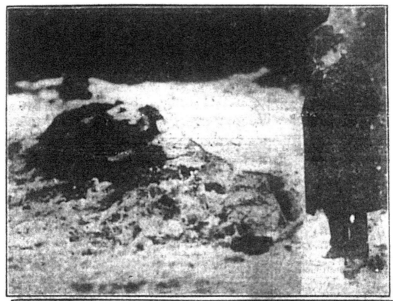

Charles Levin poses for photographer Frank T. Schauble. Also, a glimpse at Levin's Tailor shop. *From the* Dispatch-Herald.

"Get that Italian and you'll find something out maybe,"[215] Levin muttered, as he started to pace back and forth. To those present, it seemed he was obsessed that the person responsible was an individual known only as "the Italian." Levin changed course and asked the reporters to take him to Hanley's Undertaking parlor to visit the body. When they tried to argue with him, Levin only became more persistent; finally, a reporter from the *Times* took him.

Levin arrived at Hanley's Undertaking Parlor and, upon viewing the body, broke down.

Her face sustained numerous blows and was beaten almost to a pulp—to the point of her features being unrecognizable. Her nose was broken. Both of her eyes were bruised. Her teeth were knocked out. On her neck was a horrific gash.[216] Evidence on her arms and hands showed she had attempted, unsuccessfully, to fight off her attacker. A small and slender woman with little arms that "probably would have cracked under the attack of a big man,"[217] it was clear she was no match for her killer.

Levin was shown the gloves discovered at the crime scene. "And they wore these when they killed my Rachel."[218] Levin remarked to a reporter as tears filled his eyes.

Drs. Jessmond Schilling and Harry S. Falk were called to perform a postmortem of the body. Rachel Levin's autopsy report has not survived; however, we can surmise the extent of her injuries. It was determined that Levin's body bore no signs of being sexually assaulted. The neck wound, most likely caused by a knife, was not sufficient to cause death, nor were the heavy blows that were inflicted about her body—most of which appeared to have been centered on her face and head. Eventually, Schilling and Falk were able to come to the conclusion that Rachel Levin died from strangulation[219] and had been dead roughly ten to eleven hours.

Charles Levin was taken back to his shop and questioned by detectives. Levin told them that the last time he saw his wife was the day before, around noon, when she left to visit the Smelowitz family. She had not returned after the sun went down, and Levin worriedly ventured into the neighborhood, going from home to home searching for her. When asked why he didn't notify police, Levin simply told them he didn't want to cause his wife any trouble.

What about the ten-dollar bill? police asked.[220] Levin told the police he was clueless about why Rachel Levin was found with money on her, telling the police that he had no money himself and, as far as he knew, none of the friends she visited prior to her death had given her money. Additionally,

Levin painted a picture that Rachel did not appear dissatisfied with their living conditions, despite the fact that he could not provide everything he desired for her.

What of "the Italian"? police inquired. Levin sat on the bed, handling an overcoat before passing it to police.

"He brought that in this morning and asked to have me repair it so he could get it about 2 o'clock. He inquired about 'my girl' as he used to call my wife,"[221] Levin said, telling the police that his wife was showered with small gifts and candies by an infatuated Italian garbage wagon driver known as "Gebhardt." Detectives inspected the coat, noting the same color tone as that of the pair of woolen gloves found at the scene. Gebhardt, Levin remarked, worked at Erie's Municipal Department, in the city barns where mules were housed just across the street from where Rachel's body was found.

Following their questioning of Levin, detectives headed for the city municipal barns and spoke with James Tracy, superintendent of garbage collection. Police learned the "Gebhardt" was Aristid Celletti, an Italian immigrant who was one of Tracy's most reliable employees. With a positive identification of a possible suspect, police hit the ground running and began a citywide search for Celletti.

While officers made their way through nearby Jewish neighborhoods, police searched dozens of streets and alleyways for Celletti. Around 1:00 p.m., as he clocked in at the Erie municipal garbage barns, Celletti was arrested on an open charge by Detectives George Barber, Stanley Kubeja and Louis Scalise and Patrolman Brower. James Tracy remarked to reporters that he was surprised Celletti was arrested.

With their prisoner in tow, Police transported Celletti to Hanley's Undertaking Parlor to view the body of Rachel Levin. Celletti looked at the body without any emotion and denied any involvement in her death, claiming that the last time he saw her was two weeks prior. Celletti was taken to police headquarters, where he was then questioned by Chief of Police William Detzel.

Celletti, married with two children, told Detzel that on January 21, 1925, he had quit work at 3:30 p.m. and returned to his lodgings at 451 West Sixteenth Street, remaining there until that morning, when he left to report for work at the municipal barns. He claimed knew nothing of Rachel Levin's murder until he was arrested. After checking into some of his background, Detzel was satisfied that Celletti was being truthful, and he was released.

Meanwhile, near the Nickel Plate Railroad tracks overlooking the ravine where Rachel Levin's battered body was found, eleven railroad track laborers who were quartered nearby in boxcars no more than 150 feet from where the murder was committed, were arrested by Detectives Barber and Kubeja, assisted by Nickel Plate detective George Vance. All men were able to account for their whereabouts and were released from custody.

Speculation spread like wildfire through the Jewish community in Erie. The press was quick to ask coroner Hanley about the status of the impending inquest into the death of Rachel Levin. Hanley declined to provide any details, stating that he was awaiting the complete investigation by the police before proceeding.

As to the status of the investigation, the police ascertained that Rachel Levin visited the Smelowitz family around 11:00 a.m. and remained there until about 2:00 p.m. From there, Rachel walked to the residence of Samuel and Molly Kaufman, 138 West Seventeenth Street. From information police had gathered, they determined she left the Kaufman's around 7:30 p.m. This was the last reported sighting before her body was located the following morning.

It was only later that evening, after Charles Levin had been questioned downtown at police headquarters, that his fairy tale recollection of his marriage started to fall apart. The detectives' gut instinct led them to believe that Charles Levin was not being truthful about everything he knew. With numerous discrepancies and different versions of his whereabouts on the day in question, Chief Detzel ordered Levin be held overnight.

"It makes me laugh to think that I should be charged with this crime," Levin declared as he was led to a jail cell. "It's funny, I should say."[222]

A Tortured Soul Laid to Rest

Rachael Graff was born on July 10, 1898, to Abraham and Libby Graff in Cleveland, Ohio. When Rachel was just an infant, her mother died and her father remarried. From birth, she was as sickly and suffered from an intellectual disability, according to her father. Having not received much schooling in her youth, Rachel was unable to care for herself, cook or clean. When she was twenty-three years old, her father decided it would be best for her to marry, and in 1921, she met Charles Levin, a Jewish tailor from Newton Falls, Ohio.

What is known of Charles Levin is that he was born on December 25, 1880, in what is now Grodno, Belarus. He immigrated to America around

1905 and settled in Ohio. Some of the earliest records for Levin are for his first marriage on July 7, 1914, in Cleveland, Ohio, to Pepe Moshkowitz, a widow. The circumstances surrounding Levin's first marriage remain unknown, but by 1920, Levin was divorced.

Census records for 1920 show Levin owning his own tailor shop in Youngstown, Ohio. The following year, he appears to have migrated to Newton Falls, Ohio. It is unknown how he and Rachel became acquainted, but after the marriage, both Rachel and Charles Levin moved to Youngstown, Ohio. It was there that Abraham Graff became concerned with the conditions his daughter was exposed to.

In Youngstown, Levin had "rented an old tumbled down shack, filled with rats, no sewer or anything," Abraham Graff later remarked to the *Times*. "My daughter would not live in the house at first. Later she consented."[223] The reason Rachel consented, her father proclaimed, was due to Levin threatening her. "He told me himself that he had planned to murder her if she had not changed her mind and came to live with him after they were married."[224]

From the beginning, it was apparent the marriage was fractured. At times, Charles Levin was reported to have been controlling, almost to the point that he would threaten Rachel with having her jailed for talking to other men.

In 1922, Rachel Levin gave birth to a baby girl, and the family relocated with Rachel's father to Monessen, Pennsylvania. The Levin marriage continued to deteriorate, and it was not out of the ordinary for Rachel to leave her residence and run away. Soon the Levins' daughter was placed in the Gusky Home and Orphanage for Jewish Children. After the child's departure, Charles Levin advised his father-in-law that he was no longer able to support Rachel, and she subsequently moved in with her father and stepmother.[225] Charles Levin, meanwhile, set off for Erie with the hopes of improving his fortune.

It had been almost three years, and Charles Levin was still residing in Erie. An unknown skin condition affecting his hands resulted in his hospitalization for several months in Hamot Hospital, with the condition causing him to have to cover his hands with gloves. Nonetheless, this did not deter Levin, who, at his tailor shop, was hard at work on an invention he claimed would revolutionize the cleaning and pressing industry.

One night in October, when leaving his shop, Levin was attacked and gagged by four men and his machine stolen. An investigation revealed that one of his partners, Sam Rose, was believed to have been responsible for the theft. Rose was arrested on charges of larceny and brought before an Erie alderman. The machine was eventually discovered and returned to Levin and the charges dropped. Soon after, rumor spread that Charles Levin's invention could make him a millionaire, and by November Abraham Graff learned of Levin's imminent success, and a warrant was issued out of Monessen for Charles Levin's arrest for desertion.

Charles Levin was arrested and taken back to Monessen to face the charges against him. It was while in Monessen that Charles and Rachel reconciled and Levin convinced Abraham Graff to allow his daughter to return with him to Erie. Graff withdrew the charges, and in several days, Charles Levin returned to Erie with Rachel.

Despite some reports claiming Charles Levin was a leader in the Jewish community, this was anything but true. And the arrival of an unknown wife only puzzled those who looked on him with disdain. It was quite obvious that Levin was not respected in the Jewish community. A customer of Levin's remarked:

> When he came here he told us he was a single man. His wife was dead and he had a daughter fifteen or sixteen teaching in a Hebrew school. We did hear that he was going to marry again. Of course that all proved untrue. Nobody likes him very well around here. There is something queer about him. He may have a little education. Anyway, he has that invention of his. Another fellow got mixed into it and Levine tried to bluff him. That's all he did. Bluff.[226]

The brief reconciliation was short-lived, as both Rachel and Charles receded into their daily quarrels. Rachel complained about the living conditions to those who would listen. Rachel's concerns about the conditions she was exposed to were entirely valid. The living quarters was said to have consisted of

> a squalid 8 by 12 room back of the tailor shop at Twenty-first and French streets formed the living apartments of the two. A green, iron bed was their place of repose, and it wasn't any wider than the average single bed. Good, heavy comfortable clothing was on it though. Behind a curtain that shut out a view from the business place, stood the table where the folk ate their frugal meal to the hissing of the steam from a pressing machine that stood over in the other corner.[227]

As the months wore on, the arguments between husband and wife escalated. Some were so tense they caused Rachel to stay overnight with friends within the Jewish settlement to get away from her husband. On the morning of January 23, 1925, Levin asked Chief of Police Detzel for permission to attend his wife's funeral. Detzel allowed Levin to leave but reminded him he would be brought back for further questioning. Levin was placed in the care of Detectives Talbert and Doyle, and the three men left for Hanley's Undertaking Parlor.

Abraham Graff had arrived at Union Depot around five o'clock that morning, having left Monessen as soon as possible after receiving a telegram notifying him of his daughter's death. Upon his arrival, Graff was interviewed by a reporter for the *Times*. Graff said he knew who was responsible for his daughter's murder and pointed the finger of suspicion at none other than Charles Levin.

In the rear of Hanley's Undertaking Parlor, a group of roughly twenty Russian Jews gathered together, separated from Rachel's body by a curtain. Rachel lay clad in white, motionless on the slab before the mourners. Several older women, members of the Chevra Kadisha Society, prepared her for burial and, despite the savageness of her wounds, attempted to clean her up the best they could, covering her face with a thin, white veil.[228] Charles Levin paced back and forth like a caged animal while his father-in-law looked on stoically, "bearded like a patriarch."[229] Rachel's small, frail body was then lifted into the wooden coffin and clothes packed around her.

Levin and his father-in-law stood beside the coffin as men stepped forward and, with penknives, slashed the left sides of their vests—a Jewish custom that bore the symbolism of a torn heart—something they would wear for a year of mourning. A rabbi read the service as Levin sobbed to himself. Abraham Graff looked on coldly through Levin's tears, and in the background, Detectives Doyle and Talbert watched over the grieving party as the casket was carried outside.

As Abraham Graff proceeded to the exit, he was approached by Detective Doyle, who introduced himself. "The chief wants to see you this afternoon," Doyle said. "Yes, you bet I be there," Graff responded. He looked at Levin, gesturing at him, "But I see that he is there too."[230] Both Graff and Doyle spoke for several minutes before the entourage left for the Congregation Brith Shalom Cemetery on West Ridge Road.

The ride venturing out past the city limits was quiet as the caravan of vehicles pulled up to the cemetery gates, covered in ice and snow. A stinging, bitter air nipped at the mourners as they proceeded into the cemetery toward a pre-dug grave. Rachel's body was removed and lowered into the ground. Someone then stepped forward, producing a bucket carrying the bloodstained snow found around her body.

Congregation Brith Shalom Cemetery, West Ridge Road. *Author's collection.*

As the bloodied clumps of snow thudded against the coffin, a Hebrew prayer was read, and following it, the book was handed to Levin, who stood before Rachel's grave. The grave was steadily filled as Levin's voice wavered. After Levin finished, the group of men, women and children returned to their vehicles and Levin stood alone next to the grave as a stick was erected in the loose soil. Levin slowly shuffled back to the car where Detectives Doyle and Talbert stood, waiting to take him back downtown.

At police headquarters, the grilling by Chief of Police Detzel and Lieutenant of Detectives George Christoph continued, with suspicion focusing on the many discrepancies in Levin's statements to police. Police also questioned Samuel Kaufman and Clara Smelowitz to help construct a clearer understanding of Rachel's last moments in relation to Charles Levin's statements.

Not all of the detectives, however, believed that Levin was a suspect. Some, including County Detective Leroy Search, believed the theory that an African American was responsible. Although practically no evidence was ever collected to suggest such an outlandish and ridiculous theory, a small percentage of the police supported this purely by the manner in which Rachel Levin was beaten. Nevertheless, Detzel ordered his men to search for

Chief William F. "Billy" Detzel, Erie City Police. *From the* Police Journal, *June 1918.*

every clue possible that might aid in solving the mystery—regardless of the theory.

Clara Smelowitz told police Rachel Levin came to her house around 11:00 a.m., where she remained until about 2:00 p.m. Despite having a limited vocabulary, Rachel complained about her tonsils and teeth and expressed a desire to visit her father and daughter. Smelowitz tried to persuade Rachel to eat something but was unsuccessful.

After leaving the Smelowitz residence, Rachel headed for the residence of Molly and Samuel Kaufman. Molly Kaufman was absent, but Samuel told police he and his children were home and they welcomed Rachel for dinner. Later that afternoon, with the family gathered around the table after dinner, Molly Kaufman was able to coax Rachel into eating some food before she slipped into her usual melancholic depression, again expressing a desire to see her daughter and father.

"Well, why don't you go see your father and your baby?" Molly Kaufman asked Rachel. "It is not that far to go."

"But I have no money, my husband has no money to send me. I can't go, I can't go,"[231] Rachel responded.

Suddenly, Samuel Kaufman told police, around 7:00 or 7:30 p.m., Rachel told the Kaufman family she had to go home. "My husband may be angry with me if I don't go home."[232]

It was shortly after this Rachel Levin left and was never seen alive again. Kaufman told police that Charles Levin had visited his residence at both 9:00 p.m. and 1:30 a.m. searching for his wife. Kaufman suggested that Levin go to the police to report her missing. Levin also went to the Smelowitz residence in the early morning hours and was told by Adolph and Clara Smelowitz to ask the police to help him in his search.

At the same time in the investigation, the belief that Aristid Celletti had anything to do with Rachel Levin's death gradually failed to gain traction, and police soon believed that there was insufficient information to suggest that he was involved. Charles Levin, who had endured an additional several hours of grilling following his wife's funeral, was released later that day around 4:00 p.m.

As Levin left police headquarters accompanied by another man, he looked toward the police, tipped his hat, saluted and waved goodbye. As he walked south on Peach Street, one officer who witnessed the bizarre exit commented, "Hell, that guy looks as though he was going home from a baseball game, instead of having been held for two days as a murder suspect."[233]

Since the discovery of Rachel Levin's body, all members of the Detective Bureau for the City of Erie Police Department had been working nonstop to search for her killer. Police acknowledged the possibility that Charles Levin was innocent of his wife's murderer, yet they also acknowledged that at that moment they were without any tangible clues or information that would allow them to make an arrest in the case.

It was looking likely that this crime would go unsolved—that is, until ten-year-old Louise Eck came forward as a possible witness.

At about 8:00 p.m. on January 21, 1925, Louise Eck and several children had been sledding on the northern side of the Nickel Plate Railroad tracks when Louise heard a woman's scream coming from the ravine on the other side of the tracks. Immediately, Louise alerted the other children, although they chalked it up to coming from a streetcar. The scream, Eck told police and reporters, resembled a "muffled shout,"[234] as if someone was screaming for help. After the screams died down, a faint moaning sound could still be heard coming from the ravine.

Frightened, Louise attempted to flag down a passing car. but the driver paid no attention and kept on driving. Around 8:30 p.m., the sounds coming from the ravine finally ceased. After obtaining Louise Eck's statement, police believed that this was when Rachel Levin was murdered. None of the children recalled seeing any pedestrians on French Street coming from the ravine at or around the time the sounds were heard.

Later on the twenty-fourth, police uncovered an additional clue. A bundle of wastepaper was found within 150 feet of Levin's tailor shop. The bundle, stained with human blood, was presented to the police in an attempt to extract fingerprints. Unfortunately, due to the texture of the paper, when attempts were made to extract fingerprints, the prints became blotted, rendering the prints—or what was left of them—practically useless.[235]

Desperate for clues in their search for the murderer, Detective Sergeants James Barron and Louis Scalise were sent into the "Black Belt" of Erie's Second Ward in search for clues. Barron and Scalise arrested five men: Casey James (twenty-one), William McDonald (twenty-five), Merldon Henderson

CITY HALL, ERIE, PA,

Erie City Hall. *Author's collection.*

(twenty-one), Charles Davis (twenty-five) and Charles Sanders (twenty-seven). The *Erie Daily Times* acknowledged,

> *It is not believed that the police have any evidence which would actually connect any of these most recent suspects with the murder of Mrs. Levin. The round-up, however indicates that the authorities are finally turning their efforts to the support of the theory that the tailor's wife was the victim of a vicious street attack and presumably by a member of the Negro race.*[236]

The five men were released when evidence showed they were not connected with Rachel Levin's murder. Despite the fact that by 1925 Erie had become a progressive city compared to others in the country, the arrests by the Erie Police Department still highlighted divisive social beliefs that such heinous crimes were considered to be the work of African Americans.

"We have several clues which we can not give for publication," Lieutenant of Detectives Christoph admitted to the *Dispatch-Herald*. "Information which has come to us within the last 24 hours looks good and as soon as we can check up on this we will be in position to know whether or not we can lay our hands on the murderer."[237]

Additional evidence came into the hands of police that caused them to take a fresh look at the case. The more they reviewed the evidence in their possession—although circumstantial—they became further convinced Charles Levin was not being entirely truthful about his wife's death and what he knew. Charles Levin was arrested on the afternoon of January 26, 1925, on an open charge in connection with the murder of his wife.

This time, police intended to do everything they could to find the murderer and bring him to justice.

THE HUNT FOR A SUSPECT

When Charles Levin was arrested a second time, he retained the services of local attorney William Carney. Carney warned Levin to keep his mouth shut. The local press put the pressure on Levin, too, with newspapers predicting that an arrest would be made within the next twenty-four hours.

Keeping his evidence close, Christoph told reporters the information he had come across invigorated the detectives and had revived their investigation. When he arrived at police headquarters, Levin was ushered into the office of Chief Detzel. Also present were Mayor Joseph Williams, Finance Director Thomas Mehaffey and Lieutenant of Detectives Christoph.

Police revisited Levin's whereabouts and movements on the night of the twenty-first and the early morning hours of the twenty-second. It was reported the interrogation moved into the realm of the "third degree"; however, what exactly was said in Chief Detzel's office remains unknown. Police questioned Levin about the numerous misstatements he made in prior discussions with them, particularly his actions in searching for his wife.

Officer Magnus Johnson, Erie City Police. *Courtesy of the Johnson family.*

Previously, Levin remarked during his original cross-examination that at 1:30 a.m. on January 22, he spoke with a police officer at the corner of East Twenty-First and State Streets regarding a fire.[238] Police told Levin that there were major errors in his story. Although a follow-up with Officer Magnus Johnson confirmed he did briefly speak with Levin when he reported the fire at an alarm box, the timing was incorrect. In checking the records within the fire department, the fire had not been reported until 2:35 a.m.

Police also advised Levin that during his previous cross-examination he had remarked that he appeared at the Kaufman home at 1:30 a.m., but during another round of his questioning he admitted being at the Smelowitz home at the same time. Levin remained tight-lipped, giving answers such as "I don't remember," "Did I do that?" and "Did I say that?" After the long bout of questioning, Levin was returned to his cell. Along the way, he used the time to speak to reporters. Levin held on to the belief that Celletti, the Italian, was responsible for Rachel's murder. "Nobody can take it away from me. I still think it was the Italian."[239]

More peculiarly, Levin's primary concern seemed to be what the newspapers had been saying rather than being in police custody. "Have they got anything more on me today? What do they say about it now?"[240]

Just as the first time he was questioned, Levin was placed in a cell overnight and was not permitted to see or talk to anyone. The following morning, Levin awoke complaining of a poor night's sleep and remarked the cell was cold.

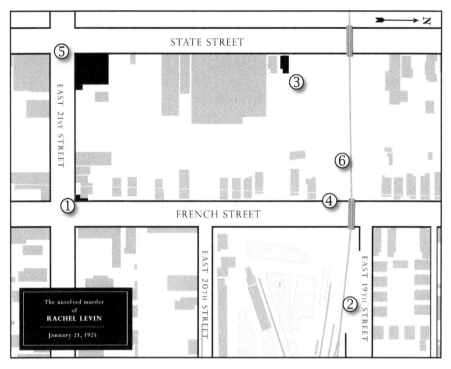

Map showing (1) Levin's Tailor shop, (2) Louise Eck, (3) Hattie Augstell, (4) Clara Platt and (5) Levin's conversation with Officer Johnson and (6) where the body was originally spotted.

Lieutenant Christoph was confident they had the right suspect. "We believe, and have believed from the first, that Levin knows a lot more about the death of his wife than he has been telling us," he said to reporters. Throughout the ordeal, however, Levin remained confident that he would be released and proclaimed his innocence proudly.

Charles Levin was released from police custody on January 27, 1925.

Leaving police headquarters, Levin spoke with reporters as they crowded around him. "I'll stay right here in Erie," Levin said defiantly, "I'm going to work on my patent and when the Buffalo people organize the company to make these machines I will be its president."[241]

Lieutenant Christoph warned that this was not the end of the investigation. "This investigation will go on until we have run down every possible angle of the case. If there is a possible solution I'm sure we will be able to find it."[242]

As the investigation reached a dead end, Dr. Jessmond Schilling took the opportunity to clear up several misconceptions that had prevailed during the early stages of the investigation, attacking the newspaper articles claiming that Rachel Levin was pregnant when she was murdered. Schilling stated that an examination did not show she was pregnant. Schilling also dispelled the notion that Levin had been sexually assaulted and confirmed that no intercourse had taken place.

As for the next steps in the investigation, police planned to trace Charles Levin's former partner, Sam Rose. However, they expressed doubt in Rose's involvement in the case upon hearing reports that he had fled to Rochester and had been there for some time following the incident with Levin in November 1924.

The last breaths in the investigation appear to have been when twenty-seven-year-old Willie White, an African American, was arrested in the Squirrel Hill neighborhood of Pittsburgh in late February. White confessed to having robbed and choked no fewer than nine women there, and police believed they could sweat a confession from him. Lieutenant of Detectives Christoph reviewed White's criminal record in Erie and any possible associations. This lead quickly sputtered out, and the case of Rachel Levin's murder slipped into the unsolved case files at the district attorney's office.

Charles Levin kept his word when he promised to remain in Erie—at least for some time. This was evident several weeks after Rachel's death when an advertisement appeared in the *Erie Daily Times* promising his invention, valued at $200,000, gained additional investors and would be welcoming individuals from New York to start a manufacturing plant. What ultimately happened to Levin's plans remain unknown, as he appears to have left Erie by 1926. What happened to him following his departure from Erie remains a mystery.

It is clear that police possessed a circumstantial case against Charles Levin. It is likely there was even more damning evidence against him that will never be known due to the files no longer existing. Levin's inability to treat the investigation and questioning against him as serious not only hindered investigators but also made them zero in on him as a particular suspect.

Most of the investigators went to their graves believing Charles Levin was responsible. If Charles Levin murdered his wife, this is what likely transpired: We know police possessed information that led them to believe that Rachel had returned to Levin's shop at 32 West Twenty-First Street. It is possible Rachel returned and found a $10 bill, which was a considerable amount even in 1925. Levin had bragged and promoted his invention as having been worth $200,000.[243] This begs the question, for an individual who claimed he had no money, by what means did he build such an expensive invention? What funds were provided? Did he have sponsors?

It's possible Rachel confronted her husband about his claim that they didn't have much money. Rachel, desperately wanting to visit her father and daughter, refused to give the money back to her husband, and an argument ensued. If Rachel went back "home," there was a chance she would not return—and also the possibility of Levin being charged or imprisoned for support or desertion. Such a risk would ruin Levin's chances of seeing his invention becoming successful.

Rachel then left, perhaps to head to the home of another Jewish family who would take her in. It was while she reached the ravine next to the steel overpass for the railroad tracks that Charles Levin caught up to her and a struggle ensued. Rachel then sustained indescribable injuries that were inflicted by someone who possessed rage. If we are to believe her father, Levin had made prior threats against his wife. Did he finally act on those threats? Ultimately, without any definitive knowledge about the background of the household and marriage before the murder happened, all of this is conjecture, of course.

Unbeknownst to Charles Levin, his wife was still alive, clinging to life as he returned to his tailor shop. While there, he possibly used the pair of gloves and handkerchiefs and, returning to the scene, staged them. It was at this moment that Levin, realizing that Rachel was still alive after being beaten and stabbed, strangled her to death.

Charles Levin's alibi is certainly useless, especially since Levin himself even remarked that the time was conflicting. Venturing into the Jewish neighborhood throughout the night and attempting to make conversation with an Erie City Police officer in the early morning were nothing more than poorly constructed attempts to account for his whereabouts and deflect attention from himself.

Further, it was known that Rachel Levin usually stayed overnight with other Jewish families whenever she and Charles had a row. Levin even confirmed it was not out of the ordinary. So what possessed Levin to suddenly search for his wife in the frantic nature he did and when approaching friends—and the police—still failed to report her missing? These acts certainly do not appear to have been that of a concerned husband doing everything possible to find his wife.

A motive is clear: Charles Levin was focused on turning his invention into a source of income that would lift him out of poverty. He was obsessed with seeing it through to completion. And the risks presented to him put his dreams on jeopardy. For Charles Levin, his wife was getting in the way of him becoming wealthy from his invention.

Although this is a theory, there is still the small chance that Rachel could have been murdered by someone who was a stranger to her. If that was the case, the fact that police were looking for someone who resembled a beast or raging lunatic or based purely on race would have made the apprehension of her killer that much harder and unrealistic.

Although he was cleared of involvement in Rachel's murder, Aristid Celletti cannot be eliminated as having been the murderer. In 1926, Celletti would be arrested on a charge of statutory rape against a seven-year-old[244] and was clearly a violent individual. This makes Celletti's remarks about Rachel resembling a child much more frightening. Celletti pleaded guilty and was sent to the Western State Penitentiary. He was released in 1929.[245] However, one must tread lightly, as the claims that Celletti doted on Rachel Levin, showering her with trinkets and gifts, came entirely from Charles Levin, and police knew these stories possibly had no truth to them at all.

As for Abraham Graff, his daughter's death haunted him the rest of his life. Although Abraham and his wife, Fannie, had money to comfortably retire for the rest of their lives, Rachel's murder changed that. Abraham was determined to see Rachel's murderer brought to justice and spent almost his entire savings searching for her killer. It was during this time that Abraham became a victim in his own manner when swindled out of his entire life savings by two men who conned him into buying several diamonds.[246]

The strain and stress were simply too much to bear, and Abraham Graff died in 1930 at Torrance State Hospital from chronic myocarditis and senility at the age of sixty-five. His wife, Fannie, died from senile dementia at Dixmont State Hospital in 1951.

One of the biggest mysteries in Rachel Levin's murder and its aftermath is what happened to her daughter. It is believed that she remained in the Gusky Orphanage, given that Rachel's parents were unable to care for her. The orphanage closed in 1943 due to the growing popularity of fostering children and extended family placements. Adoption records held in the Jewish Archives of Western Pennsylvania are restricted and sealed from the public until 2040.

Ninety-six years after the murder of Rachel Levin, the place where she met her untimely death still remains and is perhaps one of the more "preserved" crime scenes discussed in this work. The Nickel Plate Railroad tracks are long gone, having been removed in 2002. The steel bridge that carried them over French Street is gone, too. However, the embankments alongside the ravine where she was found are still there. Levin's tailor shop is long gone. The Smelowitz house still stands, whereas the Kaufman residence, where

Above: Present-day view of the murder location of Rachel Levin. Note the embankment to the right where the tracks used to be. *Author's collection.*

Left: Rachel Levin's grave. *Author's collection.*

Rachel Levin had her last meal, no longer exists. The older houses on East Seventeenth Street were replaced long ago with lower-income housing.

It's no secret that as soon as the body was discovered, Chief Detzel ordered his detectives to chase Rachel Levin's murderer to the ends of the earth, leaving no stone unturned. If anything, the inability to bring Rachel's murderer to justice was not due to negligence on behalf of the police. Like many cases from that time, the mystery remains due to a lack of evidence and forensic technology. It's almost assured that had this crime occurred today, the murderer would have been brought to justice.

Rachel Levin's grave sits nestled among a cluster of older tombstones on the grounds of the Congregation Brith Shalom Cemetery away from the now bustling West Lake Road. Her tombstone simply reads, "Rachel Graff 1898–1925."

Other words on Rachel's tombstone, written in Hebrew, show their age; the message is not entirely legible, but it bears witness to the horrible crime that occurred on January 21, 1925.

NOTES

1. Dead at the Post of Duty: The 1905 Murder of Detective Sergeant James Higgins

1. There is some dispute at the time the call came in. The *Erie Dispatch* claimed it occurred around 12:30 a.m. and that the suspicious man was seen loitering around the premises of Shaw Laundry, located opposite the Henry Shenk Company Mill.
2. "Detective Higgins Brutally Murdered!" *Erie Daily Times*, May 15, 1905.
3. Ibid.
4. Ibid
5. "Inquest Over Dead Detective," *Erie Daily Times*, May 16, 1905.
6. Ibid.
7. Ibid.
8. "Police Officer Higgins Murdered!" *Erie Dispatch*, May 14, 1905.
9. Ibid.
10. Ibid.
11. Some documents list Higgins's mother's name as Mary. Evidence as to his mother's name as being Sarah comes from the Death Index for the City of Buffalo in 1892 when his younger sister, Maria, died.
12. "Detective Higgins' Long Career," *Erie Daily Times*, May 15, 1905.
13. Ibid.
14. Schau, a tailor, shot and murdered his twenty-two-year-old daughter, Minnie, and seriously wounded another daughter, Annie. Schau fled

the residence to the Pittsburgh Docks while Annie escaped and went for help. Notified at police headquarters, Higgins would pursue Schau—unarmed—at the docks and apprehended Schau, but not before his coat had been riddled with bullets. Schau committed suicide in the county jail on February 7, 1887.

15. Bonier, seventy-five, a former resident of Erie, fled Buffalo after being accused of smashing in the faces of Franz and Johanna Freher and hiding their bodies in the shed of their residence. After a lengthy series of appeals, Bonier was executed by electrocution on July 31, 1907.

16. "Police Officer Higgins Murdered!"

17. "$1,000 Memorial Fund Proposed," *Erie Daily Times*, May 15, 1905.

18. "The Higgins Memorial Fund," *Erie Daily Times*, June 7, 1905.

19. "Detective Higgins' Long Career," *Erie Daily Times*, May 15, 1905.

20. "Detective Higgins' Murderer," *Erie Daily Times*, February 21, 1907.

21. A short crowbar or tool used by burglars to force open a window or door.

22. The valise was found by Carl Herman in Schlosser's lumberyard as Herman was heading home from church. Hearns later advised police all the contents in the valise were accounted for.

23. "Girard Suspect Was Wrong Man," *Erie Dispatch*, May 15, 1905.

24. "Inquest Over Dead Detective," *Erie Daily Times*, May 16, 1905.

25. "$2,000 Reward!" *Erie Daily Times*, May 16, 1905.

26. "Detective Higgins' Murderer," *Erie Daily Times*, February 21, 1907.

27. Ibid.

28. Ibid.

29. "He Will Answer Duty's Call No More," *Erie Daily Times*, May 17, 1905.

30. "Thousands Mourned for Officer Higgins," *Erie Daily Times*, May 18, 1905.

31. Ibid.

32. Ibid.

33. "Is Murderer Under Arrest?" *Erie Daily Times*, June 27, 1905.

34. Watson also showed the photograph to McCarthy's mother and sister, who believed that the clothes the man was wearing on the day before he was found matched McCarthy.

35. Horace L. Chapman, a wealthy coal dealer and former Democratic candidate for governor, was out of town with his family at the time. Burglar alarms had recently been installed in the Chapman mansion; these consisted of tiny threads that covered the windows. If the alarms were tampered with, it triggered an alarm to the Postal Telegraph and Cable Company.

36. At forty-eight years old, Davis was a nine-year veteran with the Columbus Police Department; he left behind a widow and son.

37. Police were able to later trace the gun as having been stolen from a man named Heineman in Dunkirk, New York.

38. Reed was eventually identified as Michael Murray.

39. Caster was previously sentenced to four years for a burglary that was committed in Kalamazoo, Michigan.

40. "Columbus Officials Have Murder Suspect," *Erie Daily Times*, August 19, 1905.

41. Ibid.

42. Ibid.

43. "Columbus Gunpowder Plot," *Cincinnati Enquirer*, August 27, 1905.

44. "Detective Higgins' Murderer," *Erie Daily Times*, February 21, 1907.

45. Further telling is that before Watson and Wagner inspected the clothing, Caster was actually still wearing the same clothes he had on at the time of Davis's murder and was asked to remove them.

46. "The Alleged Murderer of Detective Higgins Arrested," *Erie Daily Times*, September 4, 1905.

47. Ibid.

48. *Evening Republican* (Meadville, PA), December 6, 1905.

49. "Woman Would Like to Execute Castor," *Erie Daily Times*, November 21, 1906.

50. "Fred Castor Pays Awful Penalty with His Life," *Erie Daily Times*, February 15, 1907.

2. The Madman of West Lake Road: Private Detective Mary E. Holland and the Murder of Manley W. Keene

51. "Murder of Manley Keene Still at Large," *Erie Dispatch*, October 24, 1909.

52. "May Be a Clue," *Erie Daily Times*, October 25, 1909.

53. Watson later confirmed the shoeprints belonged to Keene. Additional shoeprints later located indicated the presence of another unknown individual who tracked through Keene's blood while it was still fresh.

54. The hickory club was originally reported by the press as having been bloodstained. Detective Watson later determined the stains were not human blood but chestnut burr.

55. "Melvin W. Keene Brutally Murdered on Country Road," *Erie Daily Times*, October 23, 1909.

56. "Without an Enemy," *Erie Daily Times*, October 23, 1909.
57. "Possible Enemies," *Erie Daily Times*, October 25, 1909.
58. "Murder of Manley Keene Still at Large."
59. Ibid.
60. Bova was murdered on July 4, 1908, at the intersection of West Sixteenth and Hickory by unknown gunmen. A blunder by watchman Frank Hollenbeck and the refusal of the Italian community to speak up as to who could have murdered Bova hampered Watson's investigation, and thus the murder remained unsolved.
61. The decomposing and battered bodies of Albert Damon and his sister, Jane Saterlee, were found in February 1908, on the second floor of the Peerless Moving Picture Show in Corry. Damon's stepson, John Silloway, was considered a suspect but released. Silloway's death afterward only stifled the investigation, and the case also remained unsolved.
62. "May Be a Clue," *Erie Daily Times*, October 25, 1909.
63. "Murder of Manley Keene Still at Large" *Erie Dispatch*, October 24, 1909.
64. "May Be a Clue."
65. "Finger of Suspicion Points Not to Locality of Crime But to Someone in the City," *Erie Daily Times*, October 26, 1909.
66. Ibid.
67. "Offer Reward for Capture of Murderer," *Erie Dispatch*, October 27, 1909.
68. Ibid.
69. "The Reward," *Erie Dispatch*, October 27, 1909.
70. To interrogate someone under stress or duress.
71. "Sweat a Myth," *Erie Daily Times*, October 28, 1909.
72. "Murder Developments," *Erie Dispatch*, October 28, 1909.
73. "Gossip and Theories Not Evidence," *Erie Daily Times*, October 29, 1909.
74. "Mary E. Holland of Chicago Seeks Murderer of M.W. Keene," *Erie Daily Times*, October 29, 1909.
75. "Scientific Identification," *The Gazette*, October 9, 1909.
76. "Criminals Have Little Love for This Remarkable Woman," *Detroit Free Press*, June 3, 1908.
77. "Big Newspaper Stunt Says District Attorney," *Erie Daily Times*, October 30, 1909.
78. "Chief of Police Wagner Says Times Shows Enterprise," *Erie Daily Times*, October 30, 1909.
79. Edwin Kelso was arrested in January 1909 for surety of the peace sworn against him by his father. When arrested, he was found to have an axe and

bread knife on him. After an examination by a physician regarding his sanity, he was transferred to the Warren State Hospital in Warren, Pennsylvania.

80. "Edwin Kelso Had No Part in the Murder," *Erie Dispatch*, October 31, 1909.

81. "Nothing New in Keene Case," *Erie Daily Times*, November 1, 1909.

82. "Mary Holland Unearths Startling Clue; It May Solve Murder Mystery," *Erie Daily Times*, October 30, 1909.

83. Ibid.

84. "Keene Murder Still Unsolved," *Erie Dispatch*, November 2, 1909.

85. "Public Sentiment Says Post Mortem Should Not Be Delayed," *Erie Daily Times*, November 4, 1909.

86. "The Times Is Not to Be Switched Off," *Erie Daily Times*, November 6, 1909.

87. Ibid.

88. "An Appeal to the Public," *Erie Daily Times*, November 6, 1909.

89. "District Attorney Says No Necessity for Exhuming Body," *Erie Daily Times*, November 6, 1909.

90. "Letters Pour In for Mary E. Holland," *Erie Daily Times*, November 13, 1909.

91. "Something Left," *Erie Dispatch*, November 12, 1909.

92. Ibid.

93. "Many Interviewed by Mary E. Holland," *Erie Daily Times*, November 18, 1909.

94. Ibid.

95. This was a subtle jab at the appointment of Chief of Police Wagner. When he took the position, it was reported the appointment was a political favor and he was inexperienced. At the time, William F. Detzel, who would eventually succeed Wagner as police chief, was then considered the most experienced for the position but ultimately was overlooked.

96. "Erie Italian Murdered. Cousin Accused of Crime," *Erie Daily Times*, November 26, 1909.

97. "Takes County Constable to Do Things," *Erie Daily Times*, December 2, 1909.

98. "Editorial," *Erie Daily Times*, December 4, 1909.

99. Robert Trammel, Steve Schlop, William Stragin and Milton Hudson were executed on June 20, 1921, in Bellefonte, Pennsylvania.

3. A Campaign of Terror:
The Pennsylvania Railroad Coal Trestle Bombing

100. "Big Coal Trestle Dynamited," *Erie Daily Times*, January 30, 1911.
101. The Elpiske sustained moderate damage consisting of a dent and several broken windows.
102. "Have No Clue of Wreckers of the M'Myler Dump," *Erie Dispatch*, January 31, 1909.
103. "The Dynamite Arrests," *Erie Daily Times*, April 26, 1911.
104. "Big Coal Trestle Dynamited," *Erie Daily Times*, January 30, 1911.
105. Ibid.
106. "Several Arrests at Coal Trestle," *Erie Daily Times*, February 1, 1911.
107. "Editorial," *Erie Daily Times*, February 10, 1911.
108. The Pennsylvania Railroad Coal Trestle bombing was detonated by use of a simple fuse, whereas the Los Angeles Times Bombing was detonated using a clock setup device.
109. Darrow came to learn upon reviewing the evidence that it was quite substantial and it was unlikely that an acquittal would come if the men went to trial. Darrow's reservations were expressed privately to a journalist.
110. At the time, murder and destruction of property were not considered federal crimes. The remaining defendants were charged with the crime of conspiracy to illegally transport dynamite through means of using the railroad.

4. "At the Mercy of a Desperate Gang":
The Five Mile Curve Train Robbery of 1911

111. Federal Writers Project, *Pennsylvania: A Guide to the Keystone State* (New York: Oxford University Press, 1940), 6,579.
112. The $45,000 consisted of receipts and cash on its way to the Marine National Bank, a depository of the Pennsylvania Railroad.
113. "Winicki Identified By Fireman Seachrist," *Erie Daily Times*, January 9, 1912.
114. "Railroad Men Fight Brave Battle with Bandits to Save $45,000 in Express Car," *Erie Daily Times*, July 1, 1911.
115. Ibid.
116. Dumond's posse included motorcycle officer John T. Grant, patrolman Willard Rice, William Murray and Jacob Zimmer and a reporter from the *Erie Daily Times*.

117. "Railroad Men Fight Brave Battle with Bandits."
118. Ibid.
119. "Bold Bandits Stopped Train with Red Lantern; No Desire to Wreck It," *Erie Daily Times*, July 3, 1911.
120. Ibid.
121. Ibid.
122. "Physician Treated Man Who May Have Been One of Train Bandits," *Erie Daily Times*, July 4, 1911.
123. "Detectives Are Working Hard," *Erie Daily Times*, July 5, 1911.
124. "Another Hold-Up Was Looked for Last Night," *Erie Daily Times*, July 8, 1911.
125. Inspector Verne had located a belt buckle during a search of the area. The belt buckle was said to have fit with the belt and led authorities to believe that as the bandit lifted himself over the locomotive the belt snagged on the metal, ripping the belt from the buckle.
126. "Certain He's One of P. & E. Holdup Gang," *Erie Daily Times*, August 9, 1911.
127. "Wisniewski Is Fully Identified," *Erie Daily Times*, August 10, 1911.
128. "Is Badly Injured," *Erie Daily Times*, April 12, 1902.
129. On April 11, 1902, police were called to 1416 Wallace Street after it was reported Winicki was drunk and disorderly. Officer Fletcher was called to apprehend Winicki, and upon his reaching the second floor, a fight ensued. Fletcher choked Winicki while attempting to handcuff him. Fletcher's calls for assistance were met by jeers and shouting from a nearby crowd as they cheered Winicki on. Winicki threw Fletcher down the stairs before being subdued. Fletcher would not return to work until June 1902. Winicki was fined five dollars and costs and sentenced to a term of four months in the Erie County Jail.
130. "Winicki in Trouble Before," *Erie Daily Times*, February 13, 1906.
131. "Certain He's One of P. & E. Holdup Gang," *Erie Daily Times*, August 9, 1911.
132. Present-day Grudziądz, Poland.
133. "Hold-Up Men Fired at Lieut. William Beiter," *Erie Daily Times*, August 23, 1911.
134. "At the Mercy of a Desperate Gang," *Erie Daily Times*, August 24, 1911.
135. "Kendziora Got Two Years," *Erie Daily Times*, October 25, 1911.
136. "Erie Police Have Captured Bull Trinowski," *Erie Daily Times*, December 18, 1911.
137. "Bull Trinowski to Be Arraigned," *Erie Daily Times*, December 18, 1911.

138. "Trinowski, the 'Bad Man' Does Not Dread Trial," *Erie Daily Times*, December 27, 1911.

139. "But One Erie Co. Man Among Jurors," *Erie Daily Times*, December 30, 1911.

140. "Alleged Bandits in United States Court," *Erie Daily Times*, January 8, 1912.

141. Ibid.

142. "Winicki Identified by Fireman Seachrist," *Erie Daily Times*, January 9, 1912.

143. "An Alibi Offered for the Alleged Bandits," *Erie Daily Times*, January 10, 1912.

144. Ibid.

145. "Bandits Guilty; Get 25 Years Each in Leavenworth Prison," *Erie Daily Times*, January 11, 1912.

146. "Train Bandits Start for the Penitentiary," *Erie Daily Times*, January 12, 1912.

147. "Erie Railroad Man Retiring after 50 Years," *Warren Times Mirror*, April 4, 1932.

5. *"I Don't Dare Squeal": The Blackwood Potato Patch Murder and the Unsolved Murder of Anthony Sperandeo*

148. There are some slight discrepancies in regards to the time, as some other articles indicate the body was found by the farmers around 6:45 a.m.

149. Police traced the water bottle to the Elkoro Water Company of Elk Park.

150. "Seek Three For Roadside Murder," *Erie Dispatch*, August 15, 1920.

151. In 1905, Blackwood was attacked by four men who demanded money that he had hidden on his property. When he refused to divulge the location to his money, they tortured him by setting his feet and clothes on fire. Blackwood eventually surrendered the money, and the men stole $650 and were never caught. Police had been also called to the farm in 1918 when someone was stealing pears from his orchard. Blackwood attempted to pursue the man and had been struck over the head with a rifle, which cut his scalp, causing him to lose his left eye. Blackwood remarked to reporters that he was no stranger to rough characters and death threats—which happened often due to his prosperous farm and money.

152. "Seek Three for Roadside Murder," *Erie Dispatch*, August 15, 1920.

153. "Hotel Clerk Identifies Murdered Man as H.W. Smith of Hornell, N.Y.," *Erie Daily Times*, August 16, 1920.

154. One instance of the many who came to identify the remains consisted of several neighbors of a man from a local neighborhood who was said to have threatened to leave his common-law wife and marry another. The woman, said to have been of "low repute,' had many seedy acquaintances who could have aided her in a revenge plot to kill the man. Ultimately, the theory imploded when the man was found, alive and well, in another city.

155. "Murder Car Victim 'Identified' as Four Separate Men; Police at Sea," *Erie Dispatch*, August 16, 1920.

156. Ibid.

157. "Police Face Blank Wall in Murder Case; All Clues Exposed," *Erie Daily Times*, August 17, 1920.

158. A local surgeon and physician, Flynn was acting coroner during Coroner Cardot's absence while he was out of town with his wife and children.

159. "Murder Mystery Still Unsolved; To Offer Reward," *Erie Dispatch*, August 18, 1920.

160. "Possibilities of Identification Fade with Hours," *Erie Daily Times*, August 17, 1920.

161. Undertakers at Brugger's explained the possibility the victim was murdered elsewhere. If put in a sitting position, the wounds to the man's head may have not necessarily caused blood to gush all over the place. When the body was set on fire, though, they explained that the flames would have caused gases in the veins to force blood from the open wounds.

162. "Murder Mystery Still Unsolved."

163. Ibid.

164. Italian fruit dealer Joseph Scambera was visiting his brother in Cleveland when his body, found with a bullet through the head, was located in a nearby canal in the South Park area in November 1919. Different accounts state that Scambera's body was burned. Scambera's killer—or killers—was never apprehended by Cleveland City Police, and his body was returned to Erie for burial.

165. "Authorities Feel Certain Murdered Man Is Joe Bolla," *Erie Daily Times*, August 19, 1920.

166. "Claim New Clues in Murder Case," *Erie Dispatch*, August 19, 1920.

167. "Coat of Murdered Man Is Best Clue Authorities Have," *Erie Daily Times*, August 20, 1920.

168. "Police 'Stuck' On Murder Mystery," *Erie Dispatch*, August 22, 1920.

169. "Gervasi, Thought Slain, Is Alive," *Erie Dispatch*, August 26, 1920.

170. "Italian Mysteriously Slain," *Erie Dispatch*, September 13, 1920.

171. Ibid.

172. "Mystery Surrounds Identity of Murderer of Louie Romano," *Erie Daily Times*, September 13, 1920.

173. With the assistance of Detective Sergeant Louis Scalise, the letter was translated to English; however, police later said the letter contained nothing significant in regards to any clues to the murder.

174. "Italian Mysteriously Slain," *Erie Dispatch*, September 13, 1920.

175. "Mystery Surrounds Identity of Murderer of Louie Romano," *Erie Daily Times*, September 13, 1920.

176. "May Be Link Connecting Two Murder Cases," *Erie Daily Times*, September 13, 1920.

177. Additional aliases used were Jim Diano, Tony Blanco and Romano.

178. Cardot remarked some of the wounds could have been caused by bullets passing through the trunk of the body, and it was his opinion that Sperandeo had been shot more than six times for certain and no more than twelve.

179. Police were able to locate a small address book that provided clues to the automobile thieving ring that Sperandeo was suspected of being involved with in Erie.

180. "28 Cars Found In Possession Rochester Gang," *Erie Daily Times*, September 16, 1920.

181. "Inquest Is Held into Shooting of Tony Sperandeo," *Erie Daily Times*, September 18, 1920.

182. Ibid.

183. "Police Recover 15 Stolen Autos," *Erie Dispatch*, September 21, 1920.

184. "Alleged Slayer Joseph Botta Is Given Grilling," *Erie Daily Times*, July 20, 1921.

185. U.S., World War I Draft Registration Cards, 1917–1918.

186. Ibid.

187. "Calafato Denies All Knowledge Botta Murder," *Erie Daily Times*, July 21, 1921.

188. Ibid.

189. "Can't Squeal Says Calafato," *Erie Daily Times*, July 22, 1921.

190. "Calafato Seeking Release Through Habeas Corpus," *Erie Daily Times*, July 22, 1921.

191. "Calafato Not Held for the Botta Murder," *Erie Daily Times*, September 6, 1921.

192. "Man Captured Suspected as an Auto Thief," *Buffalo Morning Express & Illustrated*, March 26, 1923.

193. "Inter-City Bandit Ring Smashed by Buffalo Arrests," *Buffalo Times*, March 26, 1923.

194. Giammanco used the surname Altadonna and was buried as Salvatore Altadonna when he died in 1933.

195. "24 Murders Here During Term of Dist. Atty Blass," *Erie Daily Times*, January 1, 1924.

196. Wiley, along with investigators, believed that this was most likely brought to the scene by those who torched   Wiley's barn, as Wiley did not keep gasoline on the farm.

197. "Key May Solve Mystery," *Erie Daily Times*, May 6, 1924.

198. "Police Baffled by Murder," *Erie Daily Times*, May 3, 1924.

199. "Key Is Latest Clue in Mystery Here," *Erie Daily Times*, May 5, 1924.

200. "Mystery Case Taken Up by State Police," *Erie Daily Times*, May 5, 1924.

201. "Link Greenville Murder Victim with Killing and Burning of Unidentified Man Here in 1920," *Erie Daily Times*, May 9, 1924.

202. "Two Pool Rooms Raided by Police," *Erie Daily Times*, March 10, 1924.

203. Ironically, Arcar, a colorful fixture in Little Italy of Erie would meet a similar fate when he was gunned down on December 25, 1925, by Leone Amedio after a dispute. After he was assaulted by Arcar, Amedio went home, retrieved a revolver and returned to the Rocco Pia Dance Hall, where he shot Arcar. Amedio was later tried and found not guilty in February 1926, having acted in self-defense.

204. "Find Erie Men in Ashtabula with Truck Load Stills," *Erie Daily Times*, December 7, 1923.

205. Louis Calafato had a criminal history, according to records then within the Erie City Police Department. Records indicate that Louis Calafato had been questioned in 1921 regarding robberies in Homestead and Pittsburgh, Pennsylvania.

206. "Seek Slayer of Cleveland Man in Erie," *Erie Daily Times*, August 27, 1927.

207 The IRS Office in Pittsburgh placed a lien of $23,560.13 against his Chestnut Street home for overdue taxes from 1929 to 1931.

208. "11 Men Indicted in Rum Violation," *Erie Daily Times*, September 20, 1938.

209. Following World War II, U.S. Senator Estes Kefauver chaired a senate committee created to investigate organized crime and exposing

corruption. This was done when politicians and business leaders across the country demanded the government investigate the growing concerns with organized crime. The committee held hearings in fourteen cities and confirmed the existence of a national crime syndicate in America.

210. "Erie Gambling Cut 70 pc.—M'Laughlin," *Erie Daily Times*, March 27, 1951.

211. "Scalise to Escape Chair; Will Face Manslaughter," *Erie Daily Times*, December 30, 1937.

6. *"Everywhere There Was Blood, Blood, Blood": The Unsolved Murder of Rachel Levin*

212. "Scene of Killing Indicates Desperate Struggle by Woman," *Erie Daily Times*, January 22, 1925.

213. Accounts of the ten-dollar bill seem to differ. The *Erie Daily Times* indicates that the dollar bill was found "clenched" in the victim's hand, whereas the *Dispatch-Herald* claims that the woman's body was on top of the ten-dollar bill. It is unknown which version of events is correct.

214. "Heard Strange Noises in Night," *Erie Daily Times*, January 22, 1925.

215. "Believe Admirer Slew Woman," *Erie Daily Times*, January 22, 1925.

216. The *Dispatch Herald* claims that Levin's neck had not one, but three cuts.

217. "Assault Was Only Motive to Crime Police Are Convinced," *Erie Daily Times*, January 22, 1925.

218. "Believe Admirer Slew Woman," *Erie Daily Times*, January 22, 1925.

219. It's likely Rachel Levin bore signs of petechiae (red spots) in her eyes, swollen lips and/or scratching and bruising around her neck, which led doctors to determine strangulation.

220. In 1925, $10 was quite a considerable amount of money, roughly $155 in today's currency.

221. "Believe Admirer Slew Woman," *Erie Daily Times*, January 22, 1925.

222. "Police Grill Levin," *Dispatch-Herald*, January 23, 1925.

223. "Slain Woman's Father Accuses Levin," *Erie Daily Times*, January 23, 1925.

224. Ibid.

225. There is some dispute regarding this. A *Dispatch-Herald* reporter claimed that once Abraham Graff learned of the deplorable conditions his daughter was exposed to, he urged her to return home to live with him and objected to her marriage to Charles Levin from that moment.

226. "Wolf Sulked at Levin's Door thru which Walked Tragedy," *Erie Daily Times*, January 23, 1925.

227. "Believe Admirer Slew Woman," *Erie Daily Times*, January 22, 1925.

228. This is a Jewish practice called the Tahara. The shroud, which covered Rachel's body, is white and expresses the "purity" Rachel Levin would have possessed in life.

229. "Tragedy of 'Hungry Heart' Ends at Cold Bleak Grave," *Erie Daily Times*, January 23, 1925.

230. "Police Grill Levin," *Dispatch-Herald*, January 23, 1925.

231. "Mentally Unbalanced, A Pawn of Fate; Mrs. Rachel Levin Went to…," *Dispatch-Herald*, January 23, 1925.

232. Ibid.

233. "Levin Jokes When Given His Release," *Erie Daily Times*, January 24, 1925.

234. "Girl Heard Moans Told Ford Driver Who Wouldn't Stop," *Erie Daily Times*, January 24, 1925.

235. Such methods of extracting fingerprints are now possible to be obtained through cyanoacrylate fuming—a chemical method used to detect latent prints on nonporous surfaces. The method allows investigators to locate a latent print and obtain the ridges through a method of being able to lift prints from the leftover residue.

236. "5 Negroes Being Held in Murder," *Erie Daily Times*, January 26, 1925.

237. "Police Find New Clue in Levin Case," *Dispatch-Herald*, January 25, 1925.

238. "Levin's Mind Blank under Third Degree," *Erie Daily Times*, January 27, 1925.

239. "Levin Certain City Employee Slew His Wife," *Dispatch Herald*, January 27, 1925.

240. Ibid.

241. "Levin Is Again Given Freedom after Quizzing," *Dispatch Herald*, January 28, 1925.

242. Ibid.

243. Adjusting for inflation, Levin's invention would be worth around $3,126,480 in today's money.

244. "Send Celletti to Workhouse," *Erie Daily Times*, September 17, 1926.

245. "Two Get Release after 'Pen' Terms," *Erie Daily Times*, August 3, 1929.

246. "Victim of Circumstances Finds Relief in Death," *Daily Republican*, February 6, 1930.

.

ABOUT THE AUTHOR

J ustin Dombrowski has been studying local history for the past fifteen years. A native of Erie, he obtained a degree from Mercyhurst University and worked as an intern with the Erie County Detective's Unit. He has worked with local historical and criminal records and files for the last ten years, specializing in genealogy research with Polish records. He has worked in the film industry since 2011, and his screenplays have been finalists in worldwide festivals and contests such as the Polish International Film Festival, Las Vegas International Film & Screenwriting, ScreenCraft Drama Competition and Top Shorts Short Film Festival, in which he was awarded Best First Time Screenwriter. He is also a co-founder of Pickwick Entertainment, an independent film production company. He lives in Erie, Pennsylvania.

Visit us at
www.historypress.com
···

Lightning Source UK Ltd.
Milton Keynes UK
UKHW020652170522
403108UK00004B/49

9 781540 252524